JOSHUA'S
Reflections

by Joseph F. Girzone

S. Dorothy Ederer

Compiled by
Dorothy K. Ederer, O.P. and Gary Riggi

Photo: Gary Pearce
Cover Design: Kelly Sandula-Gruner
Copyright: 2017

Acknowledgement

Words can't express my gratitude to Sally King and Gary and Sharon Riggi their support in sending me the material.

A special thanks to Gary Pearce, my friend and excellent photographer, who took the photo for our cover.

With deep gratitude to the best graphic artist around, Kelly Sandula-Gruner, who transformed the photo into an exquisite cover.

Madeline Carino added her special touch by contributing the graphic designs in the book.

With gratitude for the invaluable proofreading provided by Margaret von Steinen and Christopher Tremblay.

Introduction

The writings of Fr. Joseph Girzone were first introduced to me over 25 years ago by Sr. Dorothy Ederer, a Grand Rapids Dominican, at a time when she was a campus minister at St. Thomas More Parish in Kalamazoo, Michigan. Reading *Joshua* was a life-changing event for me. Fr. Joe painted a portrait of Jesus that made him relatable and approachable. Combining that image with his ability to present complex life issues in simple and understandable terms, you are given a vision of a loving and caring God who walks each step of the journey with you.

After reading *Joshua*, then subsequently every book that Fr. Joe authored, I found myself thirsting for more of his simple wisdom and gentle mentoring. The expanse of time between my reading his latest book and the release of his next one seemed like a lifetime. During one of my many visits to New York to visit my dear friend, he made me aware of his blog. For several years, he would produce one of these postings daily. They were wonderful bite-sized nuggets of life lessons and spiritual wisdom on whatever topic God nudged him to speak to that day. They were very reminiscent of his many books in that they spoke to you in such warm and comforting tones.

The selections in this book represent a portion of those meditations, and cover a myriad of topics that address many of today's concerns, struggles and questions. It is our hope that you will find them as inspiring and useful as we have. Fr. Joe has left us all an incredible legacy through his writings and talks. This book provides wonderful spiritual wisdom for which we are all eternally grateful.

Lowell Rinker
Retired Vice President, Western Michigan University
Kalamazoo, Michigan

Foreword

We hope this book connects with you in a way that allows you to better understand the compassion and ever-present spirit of Jesus in our lives. These pages are filled with such intimate writings that one can't help but think Fr. Joe knew Jesus as a cherished friend and loved one, just like the people you and I enjoy talking to as we try to solve the world's problems.

It is our hope that the words and messages you receive through this body of work of Fr. Joe's most personal conversations with Jesus will help you fall in love with Jesus on a human level and to share that love with others.

We also hope that your life will reflect your love of Jesus in a way that draws others into a longing to have a personal relationship with Him and that compels us to bring His healing and love more fully into the world. This is the Jesus Fr. Joe tried so hard to introduce to a hurting and broken world seeking the words and guidance of the Master in their lives.

Gary Riggi
Director of the Joshua Foundation

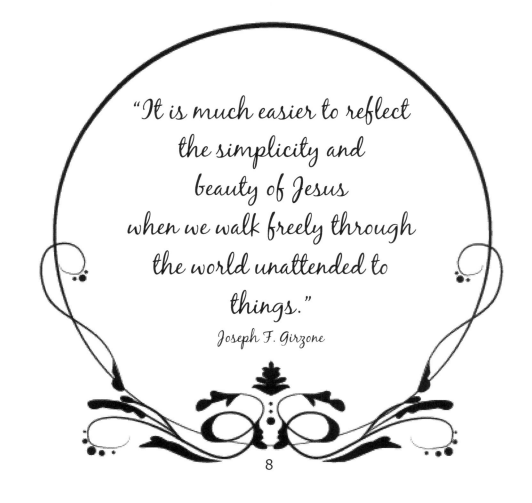

"It is much easier to reflect
the simplicity and
beauty of Jesus
when we walk freely through
the world unattended to
things."

Joseph F. Girzone

Some Unfinished Business

Jesus, now that you have Thomas back on board again, what remained to be done?

"They all had to get back to work, as they were out of money. Once they returned to Galilee the first thing they did was get their boats back in good condition and went fishing. Peter had a very large boat, so he and six others dragged the net on board and went out fishing that evening, thinking they could bring in a good catch for market by early morning.

"You know the story. They were out fishing all night and caught nothing. They were not in a very good mood by the time they returned. I made myself present on the beach and started a charcoal fire, and was roasting a large fish on it, when I heard their voices in the distance. They were a few hundred feet out on the lake. When I yelled out to them and asked them if they had caught anything, they had no idea who was calling them, and their response was colorful. They were back to their old selves. It was clear they had caught nothing, and were pestered by mosquitos all night.

"When I told them to cast the net on the right side, they did, and they filled the net with large fish. John immediately recognized me, and blurted it out. Hearing that, Peter threw on some clothes, jumped into the water and ran to shore. The others arrived in the boat dragging the net behind it.

"On shore, we put more fish on the fire, while Peter dragged the net out of the water by himself and they started counting the fish. I scratched my head wondering. Here I appear from the dead and they're wondering how many fish they caught, a hundred fifty-three large ones! We then started eating. There was enough fish and we had no problem giving bread to everyone. When we finished, I had some unfinished business with Peter. I called him aside, a little away from the others but within their hearing distance. I didn't call him Peter this time, I called him by his old name. 'Simon, son of John, do you love me more than these?' Lord, you know I love you.' 'Feed my lambs!'

Simon was hurt that I addressed him so formally, as if he was a stranger. Then I said to him a second time, 'Simon, son of John, do you love me?' 'Lord, you know that I love you.' 'Feed my sheep!' Intending to erase his three denials, I asked him a third time, 'Simon, son of John, do you love me?' Upset and ashamed, he complained, 'Lord, you know all things. You know that I love you.' 'Feed my sheep.'

"In these three professions of love for me, Simon atoned for his three denials, but it also gave me a chance to delicately set something straight with the others without making a big issue out of it, and that was the exact place of Peter in relation to the others. The meaning was clear when I distinguished between the lambs and the sheep. But when I said 'the sheep' the third time, they knew I meant the whole flock, including themselves. It was clear and I didn't have to spell it out. I knew it was a touchy subject as they were very sensitive about this issue. Some of them were very competitive.

"Then I told Peter that in the future, he would suffer, and I hinted as to how he would die. Peter noticed John eavesdropping, so he asked, 'What about him?' And I told Peter that that was none of his business. John found it hard to accept Peter as in charge. They had always been competitors, even in their fishing businesses.

"There were still details I had to discuss with them, particularly as to how I wanted them to administer the new communities once I returned to my Father. They would be totally on their own with the Holy Spirit to guide them. He would have a powerful influence on the understanding and expanding of all that I had taught them."

"An attitude of
self-importance destroys
that humility that is
necessary for a person to be a
vehicle of a divine mission."

Joseph F. Girzone

Jesus Teaches the Final Details

Jesus, what happened during the weeks that followed up to the time of your Ascension?

"They were busy days. It was necessary for the apostles to have detailed knowledge as to how to guide the community, and the communities they each founded when they went out to other countries. It was essential that they remain united when they spread out, and not just united in spirit, but in the way they were organized so they would not end up with twelve, and eventually thousands, of disorganized groups all unrelated to one another. They were to be one body, thinking together and all teaching the same things under the guidance of the Holy Spirit. To bring this about I needed to teach them some important but simple details.

"As the Father had given all authority to me, so I passed that authority and power on to them. As I passed on the Holy Spirit to them, so they had to pass on the Holy Spirit to those whom they appointed to take their place. In this way they passed on the powers and the authority to teach which I gave to them. We see the eleven apostles after Pentecost realizing that since I picked twelve apostles, they should choose someone to take Judas' place as an apostle. So, they chose Matthias. People don't take that honor and authority on themselves. So, you see when the apostles went out to other places, they all followed the same practice. You see Paul passing on the power and authority of the Holy Spirit to Timothy and Barnabas by praying over them, and as the custom grew, by the laying on of hands. In this way they had the power and authority to teach, to forgive sins, to preside at Eucharist, and elect others to succeed them. Thus the Holy Spirit would work through these men and on down to the end of time. This was the way I chose to preserve the unity of my worldwide family, all under the guiding and unifying authority of Peter, who was to serve by his example, his counsel and his authentic teaching. The others were to look to him for light and guidance in difficult and confusing times.

"This simple model was necessary, and would prove effective, because it enabled the Holy Spirit to speak with one voice in guiding my unified family. As time went on, and highly educated and intelligent Greek and Roman and Eastern philosophers accepted me as their Savior, they wanted to know all about me, who I really was, was I really God, really human, fully divine and fully human. The apostles kept telling them the basic teachings I taught them, but they depended on learned converts to translate their teachings into a fuller development of the meaning of what the apostles taught. And, that was the process by which the Holy Spirit would guide the disciples into an ever-deepening and fuller understanding of my original teachings. In time, if people are to grow they must grow in a deepening understanding of God, and the things of God. And that was to be forever the role of the Holy Spirit. That is why today in your own time you are two thousand years more advanced in understanding me and my teachings than what the earliest disciples were taught and believed, and what was written down. There is nothing new or different but just understanding in greater depth."

The Form of Worship in the New Way

Jesus, what else happened during those days after having breakfast with them at the lake shore?

"What does it say in the Acts of the Apostles? That pretty much sums it up. As I said, there were many things I needed to tell them about how they should conduct themselves, especially when they went to foreign countries. I could not leave it up to them to know how to conduct themselves. They were just going to have to trust the Holy Spirit to help them, and tell them what they must know when they are hailed before pagan courts to explain themselves. They have no experience with such things, and in their simplicity, they could upset everything, and bring discredit on their ministry. So, I had to train them on what to say and how they should conduct themselves when appearing before pagan judges.

"They stayed a while longer and then they went back to Jerusalem. There, I continued giving them further instructions about how they should conduct gatherings on a regular basis. They could attend the synagogue and the temple they were accustomed to. They gathered with the disciples on Sunday at homes of those who had enough space for everyone to feel comfortable. What I did at this home was like the Passover, when I renewed my suffering and my sacrifice to the Father. It was then that I shared with the community the spiritual food of my body and blood. This will be the new form of worship in a new way. The apostles or those ordained by them will preside at this representation of my passion, death and resurrection. Those who have been baptized will participate. There were other things I taught them at this time, and on the days that followed."

Waiting and Praying and Learning

Jesus, it just struck me how strange it is that the apostles did nothing but keep to themselves for the whole forty days after your resurrection. I would have thought that they would have been super enthusiastic about spreading your message, which you had taught them for the past three years. Other than going to Galilee to make some money and pay bills, they just seemed to have spent the time hiding, locked up in that house in Jerusalem, and praying all the time. What was their problem?

"Remember they weren't expecting me to die, and when I did die, that threw them all into confusion. They had no plan, nothing organized. They weren't high-energy salesmen; they were simple people and they had no idea whatsoever of what they should do next. They had been in my shadow for all the time they were with me, and I did all the talking, and they just listened and helped. When I died, they knew they couldn't go out and talk the way I did, so they had no idea what they were going to talk about if they did go out to preach. And, they were afraid that if they even started to do that they would be arrested immediately. Then what would they do? They were like frightened children, as mature as they were. My mother was the only one who could encourage them not to give up and go home. So, they clung to her and prayed with her most of the time, asking my Father to help them. It never even occurred to them to pray to me until my mother taught them that they should be praying to me. That troubled them and bothered their consciences. They were taught to pray to Yahweh, the Lord Adonai. It was awkward. My mother was the one who taught them all that they were to know and understand about me, and only then did they feel comfortable praying to me.

"So, if it seems odd to you that all they did was sit around, well that's what they did. They were afraid to even leave the place. Mark's father owned the house, and he was nice enough to let them stay there, out of loyalty to me. He sensed I had a plan for them. He was very wealthy, and let us all use the place. That was why you see Mark hanging around with us all the time even though he wasn't invited and wasn't one of the apostles. He was a foxy little fellow, and knew every detail of all that we did, and after I left, all that the others did. In fact, he was the first one to write, and was the most accurate of the four in recounting details.

"They stayed there in Jerusalem until Pentecost, which was a Jewish feast that took place on the fiftieth day after Passover. They had a lot to think about during all that time, and it was good for them. It gave them a chance to review the whole three past years and digest all that we had done and all that I had taught. Little by little with their daily discussions and with each one remembering things the others forgot, they could put together much of what I had taught them. In time, they were being prepared for what they were going to do. One by one things were falling into place and they were almost ready to be launched. That would take place on the Day of Pentecost, when the drama exploded, and the Holy Spirit gave them a new life."

"I have given you all you need to live happy lives. I want more than anything that you be happy."

Joseph F. Girzone

The Apostles' Forty-Day Retreat
in Preparation for Their Mission

Jesus, was there a reason why the apostles stayed in Jerusalem for all that time when they could have gone back to Galilee?

"After my baptism by John, the Spirit sent me into the desert to prepare myself for my mission. During that time, I communed with my Father and planned for what was ahead. The apostles were inspired to do the same as they prepared for the mission I had given to them. They did not have access to the Father in the same way I did, but it was important that they have a better understanding of me, and who I really was, and who could provide that understanding better than my mother? It is written that they gathered together and prayed together with some of the disciples and my mother. There were so many details of my life that she shared with them and that helped greatly in their understanding of my relationship with the Father, and the purpose of my life.

"Those days were difficult but beautiful days of retreat for them. You can imagine having my mother with them, as they were living in that large residence during all that time, and the occasions they had to question her daily about all the details of my life as I was growing up. This was something that had been missing in their knowledge of me, but these stories made them feel even closer to me, as if they were part of my family. That knowledge bonded them to me even more, because they saw how totally human and vulnerable I was. What they learned from my mother blended nicely with the image they had of me while I was with them for those three years, an image that sometimes was awesome and difficult to understand and very confusing in so many ways. And what my mother told them helped them form a softer image of me, so when they went out to tell the world about me they told about a Savior who was one of them and who was like them in every way but sin, and who loved them and would always be with them in their pain and in their joys. This new knowledge of me helped them to present to the people a Savior who was deeply concerned about every detail of their lives and who wanted to be a part of the life of each one of them. Not only was I the divine Son of God, but I was a real human being just like them and one who could understand the pain in their lives and the simple joys that made their lives bearable."

Being Prepared to Preach with Humility

Jesus, with all the training you gave the apostles why did they didn't they just go out and teach; they were successful on the first missionary journey you had sent them on?

"That's true, but remember, I was still with them at that time, and they talked to the people about me, and what made them so happy on their return was not how successful their preaching was, but how the people responded to the miracles they performed on the sick and their ability to drive out devils. Now that I was gone their security was shattered. What would they do if they found themselves out in the streets? Who would even be interested in listening to them; after all they were just simple fishermen, and one a former tax collector? They knew they weren't good speakers. They knew they couldn't speak the way I spoke. They didn't know that with me gone whether they would still have the power to work miracles. They were too scared even to try for fear of failure. And if they failed they knew they would never have the nerve to ever try again. So, they just sat around all day living in fear.

"My mother tried to help them with that as well, but they were paralyzed by their fear and no way would they even think of going out into the streets—especially under the noses of the priests and Pharisees—and talk about

Jesus. And if they did, what would they say anyway? They knew they had to preach what I had preached and they didn't even understand what I was talking about half the time. Now it finally struck them: 'How can we preach what the Master taught? Half the time we didn't even understand what he was talking about. How can we speak like him and teach the way he taught? God spoke to him and told him what to say. He told us that so many times. God doesn't speak to us, so what would we say, what would we talk about?'

"This was a big problem for the apostles. I wanted them to think about all these things, because they had to become humbled to the point where they knew they had nothing of their own to offer the people. Later on, when they did begin to preach, they knew they were prompted by the Holy Spirit to say all the things they would be saying. And, preaching sublime truths with a humble spirit will touch the people's hearts and open their minds to listen. These days were good preparation for the apostles."

What Is a Priest?

A priest is a man, one of us, like us in every way. He is also a sinner just like us. He is sometimes strong and often weak, just like us. The only thing that makes him different is an honor and responsibility imposed on him by God. A priest does not take this honor upon himself. If he does it often ends in tragedy. A priest is called by God to represent Jesus to his fellow human beings. He didn't get hooked on religion, but he takes what Jesus taught seriously, and tries in his own feeble way to know Jesus more deeply each day, so he can be Jesus to those who come to him with their pain, their sorrows, their joys, their confusion, their hopes, and their despair. Frequently poor hungry beggars come to a priest begging. He never turns them down, because he knows Jesus never turns us down when we come begging, even though we often are not deserving. Prostitutes come to a priest to share their shame and ask for forgiveness. Murderers come to his confessional and pour out their hearts over the horrible sin they committed in a fit of anger, or occasionally planned, and now tortured with guilt, hope that God will forgive them. With the power given by Jesus to the apostles and those who succeed them, a priest raises his hand in absolution and calling down the mercy of God, absolves them from their horrible sin in the name of the Father and of the Son and of the Holy Spirit. Thieves, adulterers, sexual deviants of all kinds come to him, and he counsels them and encourages them and restores them to God's grace. Crooked judges as well as the honorable ones, dishonest and despicable lawyers along with the heroic ones, mean and unjust police officers, among the many saintly ones, come to him and pour out their hearts. And hard-working men and women, struggling to support their families come to the priest and pour out their hearts asking God to forgive them for the honest mistakes they make in their hectic struggle for survival. In the name of the compassionate Jesus he restores them all to God's love. And, saintly mothers and fathers and struggling young people come and ask advice or confess their many small sins, humbly asking God's grace and forgiveness. In the middle of the night he is prompted by an inner voice to go to the hospital and visit a man in the last stages of brain cancer, and after blessing him, leaves and goes back home to bed and finds out later that the man is now home and restored to perfect health. How many times a priest is called by an inner voice and at an inconvenient time to visit someone, and annoyed, obeys the voice and arrives just in time to save a person's life or prevent a tragedy. And, how many times will a priest go to court to plead for mercy for one of his flock who has been accused of a crime and, in some cases, even succeeds in obtaining mercy. Often, the priest is called to visit those of his flock who are in prison, and encourages them to develop a deeper relationship with God, so they don't despair in their unbearable conditions. No sinner too evil and no saint too holy to be beyond the care and concern of the priest.

The greatest joy and honor for a priest is to stand at the altar and humbly call Jesus down to be with us, to become our Heavenly Food, as He takes us all and offers us to the Father with his own offering of Himself, thus consecrating all we do as we are one with him. It is the priest's honor and responsibility to be Jesus to everyone he meets, even though he goes home to an empty house and bedroom each night and pours out to God his own shame that he is a weak and sinful and unworthy representative of the Innocent and Holy Son of God. He is only too aware of his own sinfulness, and strangely, when the priest sins, there is no forgiveness. It is just cause for the delight and glee of the news media, and within minutes the whole community is aware of the priest's sins, and so many are filled with scorn, even those he forgave in God's name for the same sins.

Saint Paul's words prove to be true, "We are the off scouring of humanity," despised and rejected by the world, even though we are needed by all and give to all."

"To know what comes from the heart of God,
they must be humble to receive that understanding."

Joseph F. Girzone

What Is the Difference Between the Father and the Son?

Jesus, what is your Father like? I know when we see you we see the Father, and the beauty we see in you is a perfect reflection of the Father, but there must be some difference between you and the Father.

"That does not make sense. When you see me, you see an exact image of the Father, that is why I am the Word of God, the Image of the Father expressed in a way you can understand in some small way. When I told the parable of the Prodigal Father, who knew only understanding and compassion and forgiveness of the wayward son, and seemed not even to judge him for his obvious sinfulness, I was also describing myself. The people surrounding me then saw that same compassion and understanding in me. That was why they clung to me like frightened children. You have to remember that when I talk about Father and Son, using male terms, it is only a way of speaking, as in God there is no male or female. In our nature, there is perfection of goodness which combines the highest qualities of goodness you see in humans, both male and female. Males and females have certain qualities they need to complement the responsibilities they face when working together, especially in marriage. But in God there is no division of perfections. All goodness and beauty is balanced in perfect symmetry. At

29

times in dealing with human situations you may see a side of God's tenderness that reflects more the tenderness of a human mother. At other times and in other situations you may see a side of my Father that reflects the strong discipline of a human father trying to straighten out a son who is wandering into dangerous places. But what is certain in its manifestation is the fidelity of the Father to each one of you, as he follows you through every step of your life, like a hound, never leaving you for one second, tenaciously guarding and protecting you, and giving you the grace and strength you need to overcome the most threatening dangers driving you from within. Like a mother, he will always see good in you, no matter how bad you are, and like a strong father, he will always be there to snatch you from the brink of destruction brought on by your stupidity. And he will never give up until you are safely home."

Wandering Around Seeing New Signs of Life

Jesus, what was happening to your disciples in Judea during the forty days when the apostles were nowhere in sight for them?

"That was a problem. They were wandering listlessly asking one another about the apostles, and wondering what had happened to the Good News that had offered them so much hope. I felt a responsibility to them and visited some of them. Most of those who remained loyal to me were Judeans and some Samaritans. I spent time visiting some of them in each of the Judean villages where I had spent the last few months before my last visit to Jerusalem. I tried to raise their spirits by letting them know I had kept my promise to rise again, and that in time the apostles would be taking up the responsibilities I had given them. Those I visited passed the word around that I had truly risen as I had promised. This renewed their spirits, and they gathered in small groups on their own to keep the dream alive, until the apostles were strengthened by the Holy Spirit to go out boldly and continue their mission.

"I also noticed a change among some of the priests and the more conscientious of the Pharisees. Gamaliel was deeply affected by the rumors of my resurrection and was a quiet guiding light to others who looked to him for guidance. His age and lifelong loyalty to his beliefs presented a problem to him, and he struggled hard with his conscience over what he should do. He was later a support to the apostles when others tried to bring them to trial and punish them.

"One of Gamaliel's biggest problems was coming to terms with the difference between the image of Yahweh in the Torah and the image of the Father that Jesus presented. Jesus' image of the Father was of a loving, compassionate, humble God. The traditional image of Yahweh was a strict, demanding God who punished the disobedient and the disloyal, and had no love for the masses of those peoples from surrounding pagan lands. The stories of a ruthless God who loved his own, and only those obedient to him made an indelible impression on him, and indeed on most Jews. They did not realize that those images of God were not true images of the Father, but images painted by priests and scribes who wrote down the ancient stories of God's dealings centuries before—stories which reflected the thinking and superstitions of the simple people whom Moses led out of Egypt. When thousands died overnight from a plague or epidemic they blamed it on God, and in time gave my Father a bad reputation. Also, it was not my Father's intention that the tribes annihilate their neighbors when they entered the Promised Land. The people felt God had given them the land and the others had no right to be there, so they decided to wage war on them and destroy them. They had no idea my Father loved those people even though he had not chosen them in the same way he had chosen the Israelites. This idea was a problem for many good-intentioned Jews ever since, and presented a problem when they struggled with my understanding of my Father which I tried so hard to share with them, and which ultimately brought about my death. But, in spite of Gamaliel's struggle with this problem he eventually resolved it and came very close to a true understanding of my relationship with my Father, so much so that he was always ready to protect the apostles in carrying out their mission.

"My time spent on Earth after the resurrection was interesting as I witnessed so much change in the attitudes of many people. The ordinary people did not lose all hope and the rumors kept hope alive among them, so they were ready when the apostles finally woke up and started to live again."

Learning How Incompetent and Cowardly We Can Be without God's Wisdom and Strength

Jesus, it is hard to imagine that the apostles stayed cooped up in that house for all those weeks and never left it.

"That's because you have very little understanding of what they were like and the atmosphere in the city. The apostles were not the strong men you see later. Before they were empowered by the Holy Spirit they were not very brave at all. They may have talked big, but when it came to a crisis they would just as soon run and hide, which you see them doing now. Remember when we were in the boat during the storm and I was sound asleep. They panicked and woke me up, "Lord, we're drowning. Save us!" That was when I was with them. Now I intentionally did not stay with them, and they were left to themselves and they were in a state of daily panic, not knowing when the temple police would find out their whereabouts and come knocking on the door to arrest them. There were like children, and I am not exaggerating. When they were out fishing one day, I yelled out to them from the shore, "Children, did you catch anything." I know that bothered them when I called them that, but that's what they were like. Don't think it didn't bother me when I realized I had picked children to do such a man's job when I had chosen to entrust them with a message that was critical for the whole future of humanity.

"I intentionally stayed away from them all that time after my rising so they could live with their fears and their anxieties, and come to know how cowardly they were without my help and my strength. People whom I call to work with me and carry out a special mission for me, I cannot afford to let them think grandiose things about themselves. That kind of self-image is destructive in one who depends on me for guidance and knowledge and inspiration. If they think that what they are doing is from their own brilliance and prowess, I can no longer trust them to listen to my voice, so they become useless to me. I can use them only if they know how incompetent and ignorant they would be without the special strength and inspiration from above, because the work that I give them is not of human origin but from God's heart, and to know what comes from the heart of God, they must be humble to receive that understanding. An attitude of self-importance destroys that humility that is necessary for a person to be a vehicle of a divine mission. So, the apostles were spending this time of retreat learning that lesson in humility."

Jesus' Spirit Growing in the Hearts of the Apostles

Jesus, the apostles must have heard the rumors about your appearances to others since those appearances were numerous. Weren't they hurt?

"They had already seen me. That was a powerful experience for them. They knew that my mission was not ended, and that they still had reason to know that their own part of that mission was still alive, even though on hold. In fact, I told them they were to stay in the city and do nothing until they 'received power from on high.' That gave them hope. They did wonder why I didn't visit them occasionally, but that was good for them because it kept them humble in their realization that they didn't deserve special consideration because of their faltering faith. They would be in a much more fitting frame of mind when the time came for them to carry on their mission. They would approach it with a real servant attitude and not from an attitude of righteousness and condescension. They would be much better prepared to follow the example I gave them, the example of the humble servant who came to serve and not be served. This was the big lesson they learned, and it was my mother who impressed this on them when she explained many of the details of my life, that even though I was the Son of God, I came to be a servant, and that I had been like that even as a young boy. She told them how I used to bring troubled playmates home at the end of play asking if we could care for them, and that even as a child I could feel people's pain, and tried to comfort them. She taught the apostles much about my spirit and my understanding and was a remarkable teacher in preparing them for their mission in ways that I couldn't because they were too intimate with me, and many things I told them they didn't take seriously, and sometimes didn't even believe. She began her own mission at that time, a mission that was to last forever—the mission of developing my image in those already reborn in baptism, a mission she would have forever into the future. That is why she will always be the Mother of all the Faithful."

Why Did Jesus Have to Die to Save Us?

Jesus, did the apostles question you about why you had to die?

"No, but it was on their minds and they argued about it among themselves. They could not understand that, if I was the long-awaited Messiah, why couldn't I just declare myself the Messiah and do something dramatic to prove it and then take over. Even though I told them numerous times that I must suffer and die and then rise again, they didn't have the slightest idea of what I was talking about. They never dreamed that such a thing could happen to me, and that explains their disillusionment. Even after I had appeared to them, they struggled with the question, 'Why did it all have to happen? What was the purpose of it all?

"People today still ask the same question, and there is no way to explain it to a human. Their minds are so infinitesimal; it is impossible for them to comprehend the immensity of divine love. It's like trying to view the universe through a microscope. People, especially educated people, attach too much importance to their very limited intelligence and then pass judgment on the divine decisions as nonsensical, or irrational. That's because their limited understanding of divine love makes it impossible to make an intelligent judgment of why my Father, or I, do things.

"My dying the horrible death I endured was an act of divine love, an act that no human could possibly understand. Not only is it a mystery, but a mystery intricately tied up with human freedom. When we decided to give humans free will, it was a perilous decision. We knew all the complications and the tragedies that would evolve from such freedom, yet, we realized we had created you for happiness, and your ultimate happiness was dependent on your decision to love, not just one another, but to love God with all your being. Since love should be a free act of the will, we had no choice but to endow you with freedom to choose, free will. We knew what was going to result, and it made the whole of human life throughout your history a frightful mix of good, sometimes heroic goodness, and often vile evil, and unbearable tragedy. Moses used to say, when he reached his own 'wits end,' that my Father regretted creating humans and was on the verge of destroying the human race once and for all.

"But, that was never an option. We had made our decision. Since ultimate human happiness depended on your falling in love with God, you had to have reason to love us, and you had to know how much we loved you. That was the almost insurmountable problem. In your dense and simple intelligence, you misjudged every unpleasant thing that happened to you as a punishment from God. You refused to believe that my Father was a loving, caring God who loved you like a mother doting over her children. You refused to believe that he loved you, and your refusal to allow yourselves to be embraced by God, jeopardized your eternal happiness. Your refusal to believe bordered on hatred of my Father, which none of you would dare admit to yourselves, but that is what had happened. This expressed itself in your worship of false gods, and worship of material things, and worship of power to control others.

"Knowing how impossible it was to convince you that we loved you, we decided that I would go and live among you and be a servant to all of you. Being poor and vulnerable, I will spend my time healing the sick, giving sight to your blind, comforting the broken hearted, and giving hope to the poor. I will preach to you the immense love my Father has for all of you. I will announce to you that I had come to take your pain and your sins upon myself as the real lamb of God. I will offer myself as a sacrifice to atone for all the evil in the world from the beginning of time until the end of time.

At that point, I was arrested by my Father's own priests, turned over to the Romans, stripped naked before all my creatures, and crucified, while you all laughed at me. My mother was the only one whose faith and love never faltered or questioned. All I could think of was, 'There is no way we can prove to these creatures that we love them,' but I still asked my Father to forgive them, because they are just ignorant.

"But, fortunately, since my death and rising, a new spirit came to life in the hearts of many, and though it is like many flickering candles in a dark world, it gives us hope that there can be a future where those tiny flickering lights can pass from one to another, until, in time—God knows how long a time—

the world will turn bright and there will be understanding, forgiveness, love and peace among our family on this earth."

"Banish your fear of the future.
It will be brighter than
you can imagine.
I am still in control and
I am with you always."
Joseph F. Girzone

Peter Asked Jesus' Mother: "Who Really Is Jesus?"

Jesus, Peter's personality changed so much during those forty days before Pentecost happened. His manner and sensitivity was very much like your gentle, sensitive ways. What brought about that change?

"Of all the apostles, Peter was the most tenderhearted, even though he covered it up with his loud mouth and colorful language. He missed me deeply during those forty days. His only comfort was in spending time talking to my mother. He questioned her continually about everything concerning me and my life. Although he was inspired to say I was 'the Christ, the Son of the living God,' he didn't fully understand what he was saying. The question as to who I was troubled him continually, so he was forever asking my mother about me. One day he asked her very bluntly, 'Who really is Jesus? Is he the Messiah?' My mother was surprised but smiled kindly and said very softly, 'He is much more than the Messiah.' 'Much more than the Messiah?' Peter asked with great surprise. 'What do you mean? What more can there be?' 'You yourself said it one day,' she replied, 'when you said he was "the Christ, the Son of the Living God."' 'The prophets were also called 'sons of God,' Peter said. Then, my mother said very firmly and quietly, 'Peter, He is Emanuel, God living among us.' Totally stunned by such a revelation, Peter almost fainted. He beat his breast and began to cry, 'My God, my God, how could I not have known? How could I not have realized? It was so clear and I have been so blind.'

"Then after thanking my mother, he kissed her reverently on the forehead, and said he needed to be alone with his thoughts and to pray, and retired to his room. Since that day, all his doubts about me disappeared and his whole personality changed. He was still the same person, but he now wanted more than anything else to give up his old crude and rough ways and loose tongue. He finally realized that it was God's place he was taking when I put him in charge of the whole flock, and from that day he was determined to act as much as he possibly could the way he thought I would act, and how I would make decisions and how I would treat people. It was a shock to the others, but he kept his mouth shut and said nothing about why he had changed, treating everyone with respect and gentleness. At that they were delighted.

"Later on when Luke became a disciple, Peter took him into his confidence and shared much of what my mother had shared with him."

My Mother's Strength Became the Apostles' Strength

Jesus, in the Bible it says that your disciples were with your mother during all that time after you rose, praying continually. I am sure that their prayers were not a continuous praying for forty days. What did your apostles experience during all that long time?

"The whole time was a learning experience. It may seem difficult for you to understand, but it was difficult for me to tell them things. I had become too familiar to them, and if they didn't believe me or like what I said, they would just dismiss it as if I was untrue or it didn't make much sense to them. One thing that touched them deeply was my mother's unshakeable faith in me. Even though her heart broke over her memories of all the pain and humiliation I suffered, they did not see her pain. All they saw was how calm and serene she was, while there was fear and uncertainty all around her. My mother was a strong woman, and when I was small, I was always very sensitive and easily hurt by the unkindness and harshness of others—my mother taught me how to cope with other's meanness. That was a wonderful help to me later on, when my Father's own priests turned against me. At first I couldn't understand it, as I was always taught to honor and respect them. By that time my earthly father was dead, and when my mother witnessed their meanness, she knew it was painful for me, so she called me aside one day, and told me, and I will never forget it: 'Son, you must be strong. What is happening is not pleasing to your Father in heaven. There is a mystery happening and it is something I cannot understand, but there is a frightening change taking place in your Father's plans for you. It is important that you stay strong and not let these people upset you. You know what you are supposed to do. They may be your Father's priests, and they should be supporting you. From now on that is not your concern, stay on your course. You know what is expected of you. Do what your Father has set before you, and don't not let these people turn you away from what you know you must do.'

"This same message she gave to the apostles, and she did this not only in words but by her own unflinching confidence when she met these people on the streets and passed by them. Others cowered before them, and even though they hated and feared them, they showed them empty gestures of respect. My mother merely looked at them and would not even lower her glance, but never said a word. Her look alone stripped bared their shame. Out of shame they lowered their eyes and looked away. My mother's strength became the apostle's strength. I was always so proud of her."

The Apostles Grew During the Forty Days

Jesus, did those forty days have an effect on the apostles?

"They had a deep effect, mostly on Peter. He was the one who had to change the most as he was the one who was supposed to strengthen the faith of the others and hold them together in the future. He was growing in different ways. His temper could no longer be tolerated. It was not only unbecoming; it could be threatening to all that had to be accomplished, and it could easily destroy my whole mission by driving the group apart and creating dissention among not just the apostles, but among the disciples.

"He was also growing to be humbler. This was necessary because the other apostles didn't need an arrogant and overbearing leader to take my place. His newfound humility drew the other apostles closer to him. They found him easier to talk to, especially when he began to ask each of them their understanding and advice on various matters of concern to them all. It is always easier to work with a humble and understanding leader. It fosters gentler and warmer bonds among them, and makes for smoother working relationships, without at the same time undermining the leader's authority. And in nice ways, in subtle ways, my mother showed her respect for Peter in the presence of the others, and this was a powerful example to them. Even though I had put John in charge of caring for my mother, as long as they were all living together in such closeness, my mother and Peter spent much time talking about me and what was necessary for them all to know about me, about what was important to me, and about what it really was that people should understand about me. The apostles were tough men and not polished. My mother taught them not to confront people with a message that would already be difficult for them to understand and accept but to show respect for their slowness in understanding, reminding them that they were slow in understanding me. Being polished and kind to people would accomplish more than being impatient and gruff.

"Yes, the apostles learned a lot during those forty days of retreat and much of what they learned was through lessons my mother taught them. Try to imagine the effect she would have on you if you spent forty days with her. I had planned those forty days carefully, and at the end my apostles were very different people from what they had been."

Other Stories About What Happened on That First Day of the Week

Jesus, did any other important incidents take place during those forty days?

"Even though the rumor spread by the chief priests and the soldiers they bribed, that my body had been stolen, was believed by those who wanted to believe it, the truth reported to the chief priests also began to circulate, first among the most intimate members of the chief priests' families, then gradually to their most intimate friends, and eventually down to other priests and well-disposed Pharisees. Eventually, when the apostles finally began their mission, many of those priests and Pharisees became disciples. Also, the soldiers who accepted the bribes then spread false rumors about what happened on that first morning, could not keep the truth to themselves. They too began to tell others the truth of what really happened—that when the stone fell away from the tomb, it was already empty, as if I had just vanished right through the solid rock. That was a powerful witness to those who were open to receive and believe it.

"By the time the apostles assumed their ministry, there was already a solid group of people ready to become disciples. This group formed the solid core of the first community of disciples, the Church in Jerusalem. It was important that all these incidents happen while the apostles were nowhere to be seen, so the people could come to believe even without the apostles' testimony. They could then be an important endorsement of what the apostles themselves would be preaching when they finally arrived on the scene, after Pentecost."

The Unique Bonding of Jesus and His Mother

Jesus, was the time during those forty days difficult for your mother?

"No, I made sure of that. She had always been by my side or never far from me; I was really all she had. Her family was scattered and the woman surrounding her were strangers. My mother's whole life was totally concerned for me. From the early prophecies, she knew my life would be haunted by suffering and misunderstanding and rejection, as the priest Simeon foretold, and she would always share that suffering. Now that I was changed, I made sure she would not be alone or without me. The great mystics who experienced the divine presence within them were an awesome foretaste of the ecstasy of heaven. My mother's mystical experience of my presence with her was much more profound. The saint mystics retired to their rooms or to the quiet of their chapels when no one was around and their God became present to them. My mother experienced my presence all day long. I was always with her. It was painful for her being surrounded by the crowd in that house every waking hour. She would insist on going to the marketplace alone to be with her thoughts and shop for what was needed. The other women understood that. As she walked the street alone, she experienced my presence in a way that was much more profound than the experience of the saints. Our spirits were one and the joy she felt more than made up for my not being there bodily. We shared, we talked. I helped her understand the apostles so she could help them be more understanding and be more aware of what was before them.

"I don't think you, or any of you, will ever understand my mother. She was a special creation of my Father, created just for me. She was from a priestly family, as were her cousin Elizabeth and Zachariah. Her life on earth was isolated from others. Our thinking, our understanding of life, our values were strange to our neighbors. It made my mother realize that she would always be alone, a stranger to everyone except me. It was by my Father's decision that she existed for me. Having been educated as from a priestly family she was my teacher from my earliest days. We felt and thought alike in a way that no other mother or child could ever be so close. You people will never appreciate or understand that. Sometimes identical twins are so closely bonded that what one feels the other feels. The bond between my mother and me was deeper than that. Whatever I felt she felt, but it was as if our souls were bonded, as the souls of mystics become bonded to God. Simeon prophesied as much, though he did not understand what he was prophesying. When I died and my body was placed on my mother's lap and eventually buried, her pain was beyond description. It wrenched my own heart. And even though she believed when I prophesied my resurrection, it still did not take away her grief.

"After my rising, I made sure my mother would no longer suffer. I was with her continually in a way more intimate than what the mystics experienced.

Her soul had been pierced by the sword of Simeon's prophecy as she suffered the passion with me, and I made sure she would share the joy of my rising. She still had work to do, and that work was to mold my life in the hearts of my apostles, and from then on, do the same in the lives of all of you."

The Last Days Before Jesus Ascended

Jesus, before you ascended you did spend more time with the apostles. What was it like?

"Strangely enough, nothing changed. The apostles picked up just where they left off when I was with them before. Their big concern was when I would announce the establishment of the kingdom. I told them that was my Father's business and it was their job to go out and preach repentance and forgiveness of sin in Jerusalem, throughout Judea and Samaria, and to the ends of the earth. They could not understand that, as they preached and people accepted their message and believed, the kingdom was being established, and every place they went and preached the kingdom was growing stronger. It was difficult for them to understand what I meant by the kingdom of God on earth. The idea of a worldly kingdom had been drilled into them since childhood, so it was no use for me to try to change their understanding. As the number of converts grew, and more and more people from different areas and different countries became members, it would finally dawn on them that this vast group of followers is beginning to grow into a kingdom, a kingdom with people from every nation, a kingdom that transcended national boundaries, with everyone united under their guidance and the guidance of the Holy Spirit.

"During the last week I was with them, there were many practical details that had to be discussed. They had to work as a team with everyone following the same practices I taught them, so there would not be chaos and disagreements and twelve different churches. There had to be uniformity and continuity. So, I taught them the simple essentials for ensuring the continuity of the kingdom from one generation to the next. When they decided on a person to succeed them, each apostle would perform the same simple ritual: making sure the person was well instructed and then laying hands on the one chosen and calling down upon the person the Holy Spirit. In this way they would pass on their authority to teach, and the power to heal, and to do what I did at the Last Supper, and to be guided by the Holy Spirit in continuing all that I had taught them. So, when the apostles went out they followed those simple instructions in passing on the power and authority I gave them. No one was to presume they could take this power and authority on themselves in any other way. This was important to assure the valid continuity of my authority that I had given to them. This would provide assurance of legitimate authority until the end of time. And, for this I promised to be with them until the end of time and that the Holy Spirit would always be their teacher, bringing back to their minds all that I had taught them. In this way as time went on, the future Church would grow in an ever-deepening understanding of me, my Father, and what I taught. And since growing means change, the Church's understanding of God and understanding of my teachings would change, while the basic teachings would remain forever changeless.

"I also told them that, as needs grew, they could appoint others to perform certain tasks or ministries, and pass on to them the power to perform those tasks. The important warning which I insisted on was that they remain united, respecting one another as equals, with Peter as their guide in important matters affecting the whole community of followers. Those simple instructions were all that was necessary to send them off to establish the kingdom of heaven on earth."

What Is the Best Way to Celebrate the Resurrection?

Jesus, we are still supposed to be celebrating your Resurrection. How can we celebrate it, as awesome as it is, for forty days?

"Very simply. When you go to bed at night, and wake up the next morning, ask the Holy Spirit to prompt you to do or think something special that day which will open a new facet of your inner life that will reflect a way that I think or how I would act towards a certain kind of people in your life. There are so many different kinds of people, and you need to reflect my thinking about all those different people. Day by day you will grow just a little to become more like me in the way you think and act towards others and towards all my Father's creation. As the days pass I will become more and more alive in you, and your own life will become an expression of my Resurrection as I come to life in you. This is what is important in my disciples. When people see you they should be able to say to themselves: "When I see him I know I am seeing Jesus. This is the best way to bring my life and teachings to others, but being a living reflection of me so others will know I am real. That is the best way to celebrate my Resurrection, by making my Resurrection alive for others."

We Don't Have to Be Perfect Saints to Reflect the Risen Jesus in Our Lives

In yesterday's message on my posting for the day, some felt the suggestion made that the best way for Jesus' Resurrection to be preached is by our living and thinking like Jesus, was not possible for them. Perhaps that needs a little clarification. For us to show that Jesus is alive in us, we don't have to become like walking divine images, though there are some who already think they are in the arrogant way they treat people. What is important is that we each try in our own little way to reflect something of Jesus in our life, something that reflects what is uniquely Jesus, like these acts I have seen: when a man bent down and tied the shoes of an old homeless man standing on a corner; the police lieutenant who spent a good part of his salary each week feeding poor street people living near his precinct headquarters; or, the woman who smiled hello to a drunk on the street every day, and after two weeks he regained his confidence and she gave him a permanent job working on her estate.

To reflect the living beauty of Jesus we don't have to be perfect, just remind people of Jesus by reflecting some of His love to others. And as we grow each day to resemble Jesus more and more, people begin to see how beautiful Jesus is. I know an old priest who dresses in old clothes whom so many people look upon as odd. I don't see him as odd but as the most beautiful priest I have ever known because I can see Jesus so clearly through him. He is like a sparkling windowpane who allows the unworldliness and material poverty, as well as the treasure of Jesus' love, to shine through him. My own father was much like that. He never cared what kind of clothes he wore. They were always neat and clean, but hardly ever new. Sometimes when I was young I was ashamed that the pocket of his overcoat never stayed patched in spite of my mother's desperate attempts to sew it, and his old hat had a hole in it. My father was never ashamed of being poor, and not having nice clothes, but more people came to know and love God through that gentle, loving butcher, or meat cutter, or whatever some prefer we call him, than great preachers. Well-educated state officials and learned men and women came to him after hours to share with him their problems and their pain, while I laid down on the shelf under the counter waiting for them all to leave so we could go home for supper. I learned from my Dad what joy it is to be poor, and have to struggle. I never looked upon it as demeaning or degrading. I felt and feel closest to God when I am poorest. It is much easier to reflect the simplicity and beauty of Jesus when we walk freely through this world unattached to things. Jesus didn't feel ashamed to tell the rich Pharisee who wanted to follow him that he couldn't offer much, because he didn't even have a place to lay his head.

So, to make Jesus real to people we don't have to be perfect saints, just reflect a little more each day the beauty of Jesus to others, and his

Resurrection continually becomes real in what others see in us."

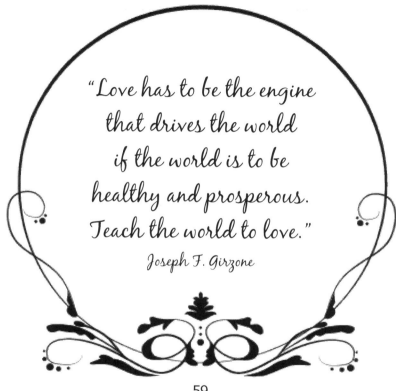

"Love has to be the engine
that drives the world
if the world is to be
healthy and prosperous.
Teach the world to love."

Joseph F. Girzone

When the Work of Creation Is Perfected, My Father's Work Will Be Completed—Not Before

Jesus, there seems to be for some a curiosity about when the world will end. You never gave even the slightest hint of when that might be.

"When my Father begins a work he always brings it to perfection. The world is nowhere near perfection. Perfection of this world consists in the transformation of all creation into unity in his Son. I am the Alpha and the Omega, the Beginning and the End of all creation according to my Father's decree. When all is transformed and centered in the Omega, creation will have reached perfection, and the work is finished. As you can easily see there is much more to be done. The work has hardly started.

"You can see dramatic changes taking place among peoples. There have always been shifts in populations, but now those shifts are massive and worldwide. People of different cultures and languages are merging. Countries are giving up their sacrosanct uniqueness and are merging with other countries which had been former enemies. Massive immigration is happening all across the world and whole populations are merging. People who were previously strangers and aliens are now becoming absorbed of necessity into other populations. Whole cultures are merging. Countries can no longer afford to live in isolation. Even the greatest find themselves needing others to survive. Poor countries are coming out of poverty and destitution and are finding that what they possess is needed by other countries. People are finding each other and finding themselves needing others for the common good of the whole human family. Groups of countries are forming economic and political blocks governed by one ruling government. Business corporations merge and form huge worldwide units. The whole world is finding itself shrinking, as people learn to realize how much they need each other. In time, people may realize that it will be necessary to have one set of laws guiding the whole world in order for all the government and economic entities to work harmoniously and to avoid continual confrontations over contradictory laws of competing countries.

This may be frightening to some, but this is a good thing because people are beginning to become responsible for one another, and realize they need each other. That is a giant step in drawing my Father's family together into one. What is needed is that my disciples rise to the occasion and make sure they fulfill their mission to be the yeast in the dough, and by the holiness of their lives make me alive in all these changes so that I can become part of this new transformation of the world, bringing all together in my love. It is the only way the world can work together peacefully, and find the peace everyone craves and prays for. Remember all things began with me as the Alpha and must in the end return to me as the Omega, the Beginning and the End of all things. My Church has been set up that way, to be worldwide with the apostles overseeing the whole human family under the guidance of the Holy Spirit."

"The whole world is finding itself shrinking, as people learn to realize how much they need each other."

Joseph F. Girzone

The Evil of Greed Even in the Midst of Natural Disasters

Jesus, what is the mystery behind all the violence in nature and the horrible human suffering that is afflicting the whole world?

"It is not the work of God, but it happens, and I am not insensitive to the pain and desolation of all whose lives have been shattered and all but destroyed. The suffering lays bare the struggle for control of all the material wealth of the world. As the Good Shepherd, I try to touch the hearts of decent people to reach out to the suffering victims of these natural disasters, but sadly, it is mostly the poor and those with moderate means who share their meager resources to help rebuild the lives of the victims. The greedy will find, even in these tragedies, a way to increase their control over even more of the country's wealth by making huge profits on the destitute and homeless.

"The greatest sickness in the world today is greed, and in the hearts of the greedy there is no room for compassion, only icy cold calculations on how to benefit from the plight of the unfortunate. The sad part of this sickness is that it is encouraged and made legal by scheming people in powerful government positions. But, the day of retribution is coming and it will come, in the darkness of night, when least expected."

"Trust me,
I am with you,
and have everything
under control."

Joseph F. Girzone

I Am Your God. I Am Not an Option That You Can Freely Look Upon as Undesirable.

Jesus, why is it necessary for us all to know and understand you?

"I know that it is difficult for many people to learn about me in any depth, but it is still important for you to continue making me known. Whether people realize it or not, the whole of creation is continuing to evolve into the ultimate purpose of its existence—the recognition of the universal authority of the Son of God. That was and is the purpose established and decreed by my Father.

"It is to the benefit of the children to understand and be close to their parents. It is essential for workers to appreciate and respect those who provide what is needed to make a living for themselves. It is even more important that they know and understand the God who made them and before whom they will appear one day for the final judgment that will determine their eternal existence.

"Knowing me is not an option. I am your God who made you and who loves you and wants nothing more than that you spend your eternity with me in complete joy and happiness. I am the Door through which you all must pass.

It is not wise to look upon me as an undesirable option. I am not an option. I am your God."

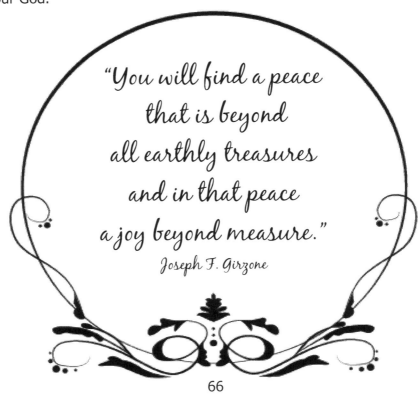

"You will find a peace
that is beyond
all earthly treasures
and in that peace
a joy beyond measure."

Joseph F. Girzone

Do Not Be Afraid of the Future!

Jesus, we are so concerned about the future. How do you see the future?

"You expect me to tell you?"

"Yes, I am beginning to understand you. It's not easy."

"You should know the answer without asking me. I have lived through many worlds and I have never lost control, nor abandoned control. Human freedom can be disturbing sometimes, and tragedies may come in all forms, but there has never been a time when life does not continue and adjust to the most frightening occurrences. What is taking place today all over, and in all parts of the earth, is cause for anxiety among you. That is because you do not trust me. You see the future as bleak and dark like a threatening storm. I see your future as bright, and all of you emerging renewed and fresh into a changed world. Many changes are happening. It's the only way you can grow. Since you all delete your memories of the past, you condemn yourselves to always starting over from the beginning as you continually face new and more complex problems with the same antiquated tools of the past. As a result, you make mistakes that damage and destroy much of what is beautiful in your lives and in your world.

"But, despite the messes you make of my creation and of each other's lives, I quietly and carefully heal and renew the smooth running of your whole world. The terrors of the night and the nightmares of the day I dispel as unnoticeably as the sunlight dispels the early morning fog. It is not you or your human geniuses who straighten out your world problems. They don't even have the breadth of wisdom or brilliance of judgment to understand the full extent and scope of the problems. When adjustments happen and the world runs smoothly again, they should know they had nothing to do with it. It is I who continually make all things new out of the continual chaos you create. If only you would trust me and know that I love you, and am always with you! But, though you are wonderful at talking, you don't really believe in me. If you did you would listen to what I have taught and depend on me and not on conflict to solve your problems. Banish your fear of the future. It will be brighter than you can imagine. I am still in control and I am with you always."

How Would We Treat Jesus if He Came into Our Midst as One of Us?

Jesus, if you came back today and looked like we do, and taught what you have always taught, how do you think you would be received?

"The same as I was received two thousand years ago. Simple, ordinary struggling people would find comfort in my words; the wealthy, who are in love with money, would find me obnoxious and a threat; clergy who are spiritual and live simply, would be overjoyed and very supportive; clergy who use their ministry as their chosen field of politics would be threatened by what I say, and together with clergy who worship the law above care for troubled and hurting sheep, would feel a need to get rid of me all over again; and people who are in love with the trappings of religion, and the traditions of the ancients, rather than with true spirituality and care for hurting, struggling people, would despise me and turn their backs on me; politicians who are concerned for the poor and the needy would embrace me, and politicians who are more concerned with money and deny there are any real poor or destitute except for those in other countries would sneer at me. Jews, who have gotten away from the prison of the law, and have substituted love of humanity, would be thrilled to find me. Muslims who already love my mother and secretly love me but are afraid to express it, would accept me and would lose their fears and would suffer death to embrace me. Face it, I have no illusions as to what is in people's hearts concerning me, though they never really look at themselves in the mirror of my eyes. There are many, and they are in the millions, who call themselves righteous; if they were to look into my eyes and see what I see in them, they would cringe at how ugly they are. And yet, I still love them and hope that one day they will accept my grace to reach out and love more unselfishly."

What Is Wrong with Our Approach to Religion?

Jesus, what is it that we are missing which makes our understanding of you so unreal?

"It is simple. You pray to me only when you need me. Examine your prayers. They are mostly asking for things, either for yourselves or others, which is good, but how would you feel if your friends talked to you only when they wanted something? I would love for people to spend time with me, just to get to know me, so we could grow close.

"There are many good people but they don't know how to be my disciples. Protestants, whether they are evangelicals or fundamentalists, they remind me of tree experts who go into the forest and spend their whole time analyzing the bark and the leaves of each tree, and when they finish they know little about the history and significance and value and meaning and mystery and spirituality of the forest and its full treasure to humanity. Protestants may analyze chapter and verse and may never get to know me. Scripture is for prayerful contemplation so the Holy Spirit can help you to put together various pieces of the puzzle so you can develop a flesh-and-blood image of me. That takes years of contemplation. Hardly anybody does that.

"Catholics are faithful to my teachings which they call doctrines, but they separate the doctrines from my person, and they center their life on church and teachings of the church. That is good, but that is only the medium of the message. I am the Message. I am your religion. Tell the people about me, and integrate doctrines as a reflection of who and what I am and what I stand for and what are my dreams for your lives. In this way you understand doctrines as a mirror of all that I am and all that you need to know about what is important to me. It is all integrated into knowledge and love of me and my Father and the Holy Spirit and the beautiful mystery of our relationship and dreams for all of you. Protestants and Catholics all have the same need to grow their faith in that way."

Two Views of Human History

Jesus, do you see the world as mostly evil, since we are all sinners?

"Not at all. If you could just get a glimpse for one second the way I see you all, you would be heartened. There is much goodness in the human heart, but there is so much hurt and pain. People struggle to be good and to rise above the burdens that weigh them down. There is good in every single human being; better in some, less good in others, but most people try. To each one I have given a special mission and each person is custom designed for that mission. In order to accomplish what I have planned, it is important sometimes that a person not have all the gifts and goodness that others have. I allow them to slip and fall, and you might be very critical, but that is not your business.

"There are some who are molded by circumstances and end up becoming very evil, sometimes because of circumstances too overwhelming for them to counter successfully, sometimes because they choose to embrace evil. But, those people are very few, even though the harm they bring upon the world destroys so many lives.

"But, looking across the whole human family, I see mostly good people struggling very hard to be good in their own simple, gentle ways, helping others in many little ways that go unnoticed by the rest of the world. The human family is beautiful and mostly good. There are more souls than people realize who rise to true heroism in the good they perform for others and never look for credit or applause or reward. The poor more than any others touch my heart most deeply because they have little, and yet they are the most generous with what they have, even though they are considered of little worth or significance to the world. To me they are precious and their place in heaven will be a shock to many who have been given much but benefit few.

To me the human family and the whole expanse of human history is like a vast tapestry. You see the back of the tapestry and say, 'How hideous!' I look at the front and say, 'How beautiful!'"

The Worst Kind of Sinners

Jesus, what kind of sinners do you judge the most obnoxious?

"The self-righteous who wring their hands in glee at seeing other sinners treated inhumanely and degraded by the self-righteous. Sinners are human beings needing redemption, not contempt and hatred. The self-righteous are a living denial of all that I am."

Patriots Are an Inspiration to Us All

I was deeply moved by the unselfish heroism of so many men and women who, with extraordinary selflessness, saved others by sacrificing their own lives. At Mass this morning, I prayed for them and all their comrades of whatever country they belong. We are all in debt to these brave people.

As we honor them, we cannot help but think of what a beautiful and noble virtue patriotism really is. We admire and cherish those who truly and nobly love and honor the highest ideals of that awesome virtue. They are an inspiration to all of us.

I recently received an email from a dear friend, a high-ranking army officer in charge of the vast team of psychiatrists working with our severely damaged heroes. He retired recently, but because of the great demand for his healing gifts, he still dedicates untold hours trying to heal those broken in mind and spirit. He knows I pray daily for him and those he tries so hard to heal, and he has made me aware of all the pain of so many. I know he loses much sleep in his relentless concern for those in his care. He is a true hero, and I am so proud that he is my friend.

There are also some patriots for whom no sacrifice is too great, no physical or intellectual exertion too strenuous, no amount of intensive research to taxing, no pursuit of powerful stories too painstaking, in their continuous and undying effort to destroy their president, simply because he belongs to a different political party. They call themselves patriots, they look upon themselves as patriots, they proudly honor the flag, and they have little metal flags on their shirts or lapels, but they dishonor the memory of the true and authentic patriots we honor today. No true patriot would do all in his power to destroy a president. And we pray for them as well, that one day they may look in the mirror of God's eyes and see what God sees in their hearts. And I write this because it pains me deeply that I receive so many emails daily from these people, some of them dear friends for so many years."

What Is It Like to Be God?

Jesus, what is it like being God?

"What possesses you to come up with such questions?"

I am alone all the time and all I do is think.

"If you really want to know, it is not easy. You people with your theological theories think that I am without emotion and feeling and live an eternity of boring sameness where nothing exciting ever happens, and all I do is sit on a throne as people dote on me and sing psalms and hymns and praise me all day long. I would never put up with anything like that. People come here to be happy and enjoy each other and the exciting life here, not to sing hymns and play harps.

"I will tell you where I spend most of my time. It is with you. I wander through your world day and night caring for you all, and concerned about all that happens in your lives. I live your joys and heartaches and try quietly, if you let me, which is not often, to solve the messes you make out of your lives. You might think that is wonderful, and it is, but it is painful because I love you all so much and as I walk through your lives each day almost everyone ignores me and hardly anyone thinks of me. That wouldn't hurt so much if I didn't love you as much as I do.

"Occasionally, I drift back and forth between your world and heaven, since they are not really separated. In heaven I always receive a warm welcome, and they are always so happy when I am with them. They were not that way before but having come home they now realize what is real and important and know how much I mean to them, so they are much different than before.

"However, I would rather be with you all in your world because I know you need me, and it gives me joy to heal you and help you. I am happy when you help people to know me and love me. Teach them that all they have to do is close their eyes for a few seconds frequently during the day, and know that I am right there with them. That simple acknowledgement of my presence means so much to me. It only takes a few seconds, and just knowing that they are thinking of me shows me they care. I am not like a feeling less corpse. I am a living, vibrant and exciting reality, full of life and joy and wanting so much to be a living part of your lives. Just letting me know you care is all that matters."

Which Do We Really Trust: War or God?

Jesus, I cannot get the thought out of my mind of suffering people in the military.

"I am trying to press it indelibly into your mind. War is evil. There is nothing that pains me more than when Christians prefer to kill as a way to solve problems. These are our children created with infinite love and you kill them. Ask yourself, 'What did you solve by this war?' You went to war to prevent more events like those that happened in New York ten years ago. Did your two wars accomplish that? There were close to 750,000 deaths among all those Americans, and their allies, including the Iraqis and the Afghanis. Besides those killed, there were more than 1,000,000 who have suffered permanent damage—physically, mentally, and emotionally—and worse of all brain damage, from which more than half will never fully recover. If there were 100 events occurring in your country like the ones that occurred in New York, even that would have been nowhere as devastating as the casualties of these wars. Don't your hearts break over the tens of thousands of those brave self-sacrificing men and women and their families whose lives will never be the same because of that horrible desecration of their bodies and souls.

"And it is all due to your lack of trust in me. You place more trust in the brute force of arms than you place in your God. Over and over you continue to pay the price for your lack of trust. You feel deep in your hearts that I am dead, and I make no real difference in your life. You can do a better job leaving me out, while making believe to yourselves that you really don't leave me out by saying token prayers for my help, which you really don't believe in anyway. Your prayers are such a sham. You pray to me and you go to war as if you don't really believe I can do anything. If I were one of you I would get sick to my stomach.

"That's why I am not letting you be free of this troubling thought, because it troubles me day and night, and if it troubles you enough, you can then become a little voice in the night."

Thanks, Jesus. I am going to try to go to sleep now.

My Creation Is My Gift to You

Jesus, your creation is so full of wonder.

"It is an expression of Our love for all of you. You may think of yourselves as insignificant, but you are precious because We love you. Your world is beautiful because we took special care to make sure we gave you a home that you would enjoy and see Our love and goodness and beauty reflected everywhere.

"When you walk along the ocean shore you are impressed with the immensity of that vast body of water teeming with life. You could all live off that ocean if you had to. And when you look up at the sky, especially at night, you stand in wonder as you contemplate the far reaches of that hard-to-imagine, limitless universe. When you visit Niagara Falls, you see the vast power contained in those rushing waters as they make possible warmth from the cold in winter and cool air in the summer. And, the soft blue sky was designed so you would find rest and joy and serenity when you contemplate it. Imagine if the sky was always purple, or red; it would drive you out of your minds. And the magic of the plant world; just think how many different kinds of plants there are that are not only beautiful, but healthy to eat, and the endless variety to please the taste and preferences of all of you.

The greatest creation of all was human love, with the hope that you could find someone whom you could love and who could love you and you would find your happiness, not in thinking of yourselves, but in thinking of each other and understanding each other and anticipating each other's needs, and always being there for each other.

"We created the world as a gift for you to enjoy. Enjoy it, but don't mistake it for heaven. You learn by showing your appreciation for all the love I lavish upon you daily that manifests so vividly in the many little miracles that surround you each day. Enjoy my gift to you and be refreshed daily by the contemplation of all the wonders that lie spread out before you."

Jesus Ascended!!!

Jesus, where did you go when you ascended? It says in scripture you went up. Where did you go?

"No place."
No place? But, you left.
"I did?"
"My work was done, so I returned."
To where?
"To where I could still be with you but in such a way I would not deprive you of living by faith."
But, where was that?
"Out of sight."
What does that mean?
"Did you ever babysit for a houseful of overactive children?"
Sort of.
"How did you feel when the day was ended or the parents came home?"
Drained and stressed out.
"Remember when the lady with the female problem who touched my robe, and I remarked that I felt power drain out of me?"
Yes.

"Well, every moment of each day was filled with healings and comforting and listening and was very draining and stressful, so in a way I was glad when my work was done. I loved being among you, but it was not easy. Just think how you feel at the end of the day when you work hard."

So, where did you go.

"Nowhere. Remember I said I am leaving but I will not leave you orphans. I will still be with you?"

Yes, but what does that mean?

"You make me laugh. You don't give up, do you?"

Never have.

"I just passed into another dimension, which is in the same space. I left but was still there. It was just they could no longer see me. Heaven is all around you. You all live and move and exist in me; you just can no longer see me, but I am still with you."

You mean when you ascended you didn't go anyplace.

"That's right."

Very interesting.

"I was honest. I did leave and I was still with you, as I said I would be."

You know, you are a funny God. You like to play, don't you? It is fun getting to know you as you really are.

"You're learning. See, I'm real. Bye, I'm leaving."

I know you're not going anyplace. You're fun. I'm beginning to like you more."

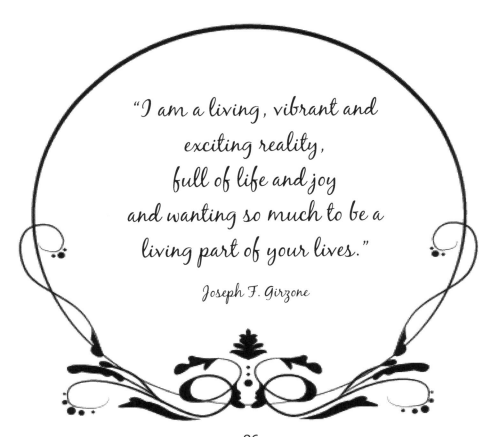

"I am a living, vibrant and
exciting reality,
full of life and joy
and wanting so much to be a
living part of your lives."

Joseph F. Girzone

86

Last-Minute Instructions.

Jesus, Luke wrote that you talked about the Kingdom of God to the apostles before you ascended

"It was important that when they went out to spread the Word that they all taught and administered to the churches in the same way. It was necessary that they do things in a uniform way and that they be united in faith and practice. When they appointed others to guide the churches after they went on to preach in other places, I gave them instructions as to what they should do. They were to prepare them with solid teaching, and while laying hands on their heads they were to call down the Holy Spirit upon them. In this way they passed on their successors the authority to teach and the power to heal, forgive and to call down my presence at the breaking of bread. And where there were questions and problems they were to refer them to the Rock, Peter, as he came to be called. They all were to follow those simple instructions. It was necessary because unity of practice and belief and worship was the trademark of their identity with me. They were all to be one in me, even as the Father and I are one, so that the entire world would recognize that I have sent them. It was a simple instruction, but it was the solid structure that would still be valid even as the Church spread throughout the whole world.

"With that done, it was time to go, so the Holy Spirit could come down upon them and fire their failing hearts and inspire them with what they were to say to make me alive to the world."

Mother Mary's Life After Jesus Left

Jesus, what was life like for your mother when you left.

"Seeing me dying broke her heart. As I looked down at her from the cross, her suffering was almost more than I could bear. She had suffered so much because of the hatred of my people. When I died, I was aware of how devastated she was; I was all she had in her life. She was created especially for me, and when I was no more, no human could ever understand the depth of her devastation. Her whole world turned into an extended darkest night. But, she was a strong woman and in spite of her own terrible desolation, she remained strong for my apostles who depended on her strength.

"After my ascension, my first concern was for my mother. The bond between my mother and I was far beyond that of any other creature, human or angelic. When I told my apostles that I would be with them, she understood what I meant even though I was leaving. But, I made sure my mother would never suffer the loss of my presence again. So, even though she was continually with the apostles and the others in the group, when she retired to her room, I often became present to her in a very special way. It was not continuous because that would have been too exhausting for her. She was the first of the Christian mystics. Many of the saints from earliest days experienced the mystical intimacy of my presence, but my mother's experience was the most beautiful and profound. During my life on earth, she always knew I was a special son of God, but I withheld from her the knowledge of my divinity. That would have been too much of a burden for her to have to carry, knowing that her son was God. How could a mother handle such a realization? But, after my ascension, when I became present to her in her ecstasies, she knew then and finally realized that I was her God. She was so overwhelmed at first, not understanding what was happening to her, but then realized for the first time the awesome role she shared in the salvation of my Father's earthly family. Her humility at that realization was even more beautiful. She was in awe at the humility of God to use such a simple soul as she to be the mother of his Son.

"I was so happy that I could make my mother happy by becoming present to her now so frequently, knowing how much pain she experienced all her life because of me. I finally was able to take Simeon's sword from her heart, and from that time on I was always with her, until the night I finally took her home with me to share the joy of my presence forever. If only people could appreciate all that my mother means to me, and that she is now their mother, too!"

Did Jesus' Mother Die?

Jesus, did your mother die, and if she did, was she buried? What happened to her?

"How do you think up these things? If she died, her burial place would have been preserved as a sacred shrine that would still exist and be visited today, just like the place where she lived with Saint John. What do you think I am, to even think that I would let my mother's body decompose? It was the sacred living temple of God, and I treated it as such. When she closed her eyes I took her home. Would you do any less for your mother if you had the power? Strange that nobody had any problem with Enoch or Elijah being taken up when their life ended. Think with your heart not with your head in such things."

The Fate of Our Bodies After Death

Jesus, what happens to our bodies when we die, I mean, afterwards?

"Remember, after my death many people who had died were seen walking around Jerusalem. That was allowed to open people's minds to the possibility and reality of resurrection. They did not return to their families and their appearance was temporary. Their bodies were the kind of bodies the just will have after arriving in my Father's home. Their bodies will be glorified bodies without the burdens of biological bodies.

"I had told the apostles at the Last Supper that I would no longer eat with them the Passover until we eat it again in the Kingdom of heaven. I also said I would no longer drink with them the fruit of the vine until we drink it anew in the Kingdom of heaven.

"The soul is like an angel, but different than an angel in that it was created to be the principle of life for a human body. While on earth, the body is the vehicle through which the soul functions, so it will share the same destiny as the soul after death. It experienced the pain and suffering and the burden of the struggle for holiness, so it will share the reward of that struggle in the kingdom of my Father."

There Is Nothing More Senseless than Worry and Anxiety

Jesus, there are so many things that can happen to each of us. It is impossible for us not to worry.

"I am going to say only one thing: Do not be afraid of anything that can happen to you. No matter what it is that may happen there is nothing we cannot handle. I have very complex plans for all of you, and sometimes there are things that must happen which may be frightening but necessary for other good things to take place. Know that I will always prepare you beforehand, so no matter what happens you will be ready. I don't ask anything of anybody that is beyond their strength, so, never be afraid, and stop worrying! That's all I am going to say, "Stop worrying! I am with you always, and even after the blackest nights, comes the brightest dawns. What I plan is for your strength and for your growth, and for some, their heroism. It may appear to be frightening, but it is only any illusion. Trust me. I am with you and have everything under control."

Will Our Bodies Be Different After We Are Raised?

Jesus, when the bodies of those who rise are glorified, will they be recognizable as the same bodies, or will they be different?

"In the resurrection, all will be changed. It seems nobody is happy with the way they look because no one is physically perfect or totally beautiful. In heaven, all is transformed and restored to its beauty before it was marred by imperfections. So, the bodies of those who rise and are glorified will remark: 'This is the real me. I can still recognize me, but I am so beautiful. I really like me.' No one has to worry about coming to heaven and having to look in the mirror and see for all eternity their old self whom they didn't like. But, I can't say as much for the other place."

Preparing for the Coming of the Holy Spirit

Jesus, how do we prepare ourselves for the Feast of Pentecost?

"The liturgy throughout the year activates the process of redemption and becomes a living force in the lives of those who participate. On Pentecost the Holy Spirit becomes present in a very special way for those whose hearts and minds are open to his presence and his grace. The best way to prepare is to spend time before the feast arrives pondering your own relationship with the Holy Spirit, and what is presently important in your life. Does what is important to you draw you closer to me, or am I in the way of your interests and your dreams? If I am, and that is the way you want to live, then the Holy Spirit will not force his gifts upon you, and you will walk past him empty of the treasures he wants to share with you. If you can find it in your heart to make a generous act of openness to the Holy Spirit and can express with a full heart:

'Divine Spirit of Wisdom and Love, I am your creation and your child. I offer my heart and soul to you so you can be my guide, my companion, my partner and my strength. I know you made me to accomplish something special in my life that no one else can accomplish but me. My heart is open to your guidance and inspiration, and with your light and your strength I will follow wherever you lead me.'

If you can make that commitment as you celebrate the coming of the Holy Spirit, it will change your life. You will experience an adventure you never imagined possible."

Be Not Afraid to Open Your Heart to God!

Jesus, as the time approaches for Pentecost, why is it that I am expected to commit my life to God?

"You don't have to—you have free will—but life out there is very lonely. You can go out and do your dance for whatever audience you may find for your stage. But, watch, and you will soon that see your audience will come and go. In time, you will learn you mean nothing more to them than their entertainment. You will go to your home alone. And even at home, the deepest and most secret part of yourself you can share with no one. Friends, even the closest and those to whom you are most committed, eventually wander or are taken from you. In the end, you will finally realize that you belong to no one."

"That is why I send the Holy Spirit to befriend you. It is not a burden I impose on you. The Holy Spirit is my Gift to you so you will never be alone. It is his role to cultivate our friendship with you, so you and I can be together as you go through life. I created you and you are mine, and if you want me, I am yours. Doesn't that make you feel proud that I am your friend and that I want you to be my friend? I don't want you to look upon that as a burden that I want to be your friend. It is just that I know you need me as a companion throughout your life. You are a special creation with a very special mission to accomplish for me. I have given you all you need to do that special work, and the Holy Spirit will be your constant companion, as will I. You will never be alone. That is why Pentecost is so important. It is your chance to open your heart to us so we can be part of your life, your partners."

"When you go out onto the stage of your life then, you are not going out alone. You are on a mission, and that mission is to bring my message and my love and caring into the lives of others. You will enrich the lives of everyone you meet. Some will appreciate you and what you do for them. Some will never even realize what you do for them. But, that's all right. They didn't realize or appreciate all that I did for them either. What is important is that you have me, and my Father and my Holy Spirit, and we have each other. With us you need nothing more. You will find that in having God within you that you have everything. You will find a peace that is beyond all earthly treasures and in that peace, a joy beyond measure. Do not be afraid to open your heart to the Holy Spirit so he can fill your life with his blessings."

The Birthday of the Church

Jesus, today seems to be the climax, a dramatic climax, of what was happening during the past fifty days.

"Few realize how busy I was during those fifty days. I didn't just disappear. I spent most of the time training the apostles for what they had to do when I finally left them. I had to explain all the details of how they should lay the groundwork for their ministry and how they should relate to one another once the Church began to grow. It had to be carefully organized and administered. They had no idea what would unfold, so I had to prepare them for the miraculous expansion of their ministry which would very soon spread to other countries. They had no experience at, or even a sense of, administering a Church which would soon become international.
"Pentecost was the miraculous burst of energy from the Holy Spirit as the Church was thrust upon the world on that day. Pentecost was the day the Church was born. And as the Holy Spirit fell upon the apostles and anointed them with an abundance of supernatural gifts, their whole life changed. They lost their fears and their paralyzing anxieties, and boldly went outside the house where they were staying to meet the vast crowd that had been drawn by the loud noise, like a powerful windstorm to the open space around the house. There was on that occasion over 5,000 people who had gathered.

"Peter exercised his authority on that day and stood before that large crowd. All his fear had disappeared and he spoke boldly about my life, my teachings, and my resurrection, which was witnessed by many reputable persons. The crowd was deeply moved, especially at realizing that Peter was speaking in Aramaic, but they understood him in their own languages. The people there were from over a dozen different countries, all with different languages. The response of the crowd was immediate and a great number of them became believers and were baptized. On that occasion alone over 3,000 people became disciples. That was the Church's glorious beginning."

The Role of the Holy Spirit Is Two-Fold

Jesus, what is the role of the Holy Spirit—the role you gave him when you sent him to guide the Apostles until the end of time?

"It was a two-fold role; to make me alive in the Church, and to make me alive in the lives of each one of you. I and the Church are one. The Church is me. The Church is my living presence in the world. The Church is the womb that conceives and infuses my life into each one who is baptized. In baptism, it is with my life that you are reborn, through the Church and by the power of the Holy Spirit. And when you are reborn, you are given a mission, a special role to carry out in the life of the Church and in that part of the world where you find yourself. As you grow, you are continually blessed with gifts from the Spirit that prepare you for that role. Throughout your young years as you grow you are being molded by the Spirit to fit you for that special work. When you reach an age when you can do your own thinking, and make your own decisions, it is important that you make a conscious commitment to allow the Holy Spirit to continue that work within you. He will never force you against your will to follow where he leads. But, still your future depends on your decision. You can live your life independently and forge your own way through life, and like going through a jungle without a guide, take wrong paths, and stumble in the dark and get lost along the way. You can also choose to accept the Holy Spirit and allow the Holy Spirit to be your partner. If you open your heart to him he will then become your guide and your strength, and as each day passes, your life will unfold as a beautiful adventure. You may not understand right away how the Holy Spirit is guiding you or where the path is leading, but in time you will see that there was a carefully designed plan that he had for you all along, and you still stand in awe at how beautifully your life had been so carefully planned.

"And it is the same with the Church. The Church is all the baptized living in the world and united in belief and in love with the apostles and Peter still preaching my message to each new generation that comes into being. The Holy Spirit speaks through the present-day apostles, who are the pope and the bishops. They guide not just the Church, but like a powerful light in the darkness they make my teachings and my vision of what life can be like clear to all of civilization, constantly lighting the way for humanity to follow through the dangers and perils that threaten the world. Unfortunately, not too many listen, but the brilliant light is still there shining brightly in the darkness. Sometimes, it is only through the little lights of individuals who allow me to shine through their lives that I can become alive in little corners of the world here and there. And in time the light from those dedicated souls spreads gradually to other parts of the world, so still my presence can reach others, if only at a much slower pace.

"But, the Holy Spirit is insistent. He will never allow the world to wander towards its destruction. Although it may seem that the world ignores him, the power of the Spirit is omnipotent, and against all the opposition from changing moral fashions and dangerous pitfalls, the Holy Spirit powerfully steers the course of world events, keeping civilization on a course that will ultimately find itself in harmony with my plans for your destiny. I am the Alpha and the Omega. I am the beginning and I will be the end of all things. The divine will can never be frustrated. My plan for humanity is glorious and awesome in its beauty and magnificence, and it will be accomplished, by the powerful guidance of the Holy Spirit. That is the Spirit's role in the world, and it will be done through the Church and through each one of you."

What Does the Holy Spirit Mean to Me?

Jesus, what is the Holy Spirit to us?

"He is the guardian and protector of your soul. He is the treasurer of all your gifts. He is the healer of all your wounds. He is the refreshment of your weary, failing spirit. He is your companion along life's lonely road. He is your dogged persistence when you are tempted to give up. He is your enthusiasm when you are shown a new path. He is your wisdom when confronted with conflicting values. He is your prudence when faced with difficult, dangerous choices. He is the brilliant light pointing carefully the way through a dark and tangled jungle. He is the cool refreshing breeze in the heat of life's threatening firestorms. He is the poetry in the voice of God speaking to you. He is your hope when all seems lost. He is your patience when you are most desperate to escape from life. He is compassion when all others fail you. He is the love that inspires you to reach out to others. He is the profound insight into others' lives that inspire you to understand and forgive. He is the living presence of the divine that resides in your breast and bonds you to your Creator. He is the unrelenting and faithful guide who leads you gently every day of your life until he finally brings you home when your pilgrimage is ended."

Your Trust Is So Feeble

Jesus, there seems to be a general hopelessness among us about the future. We are so buffeted by storms from within and without.

"Stop worrying. Don't you have any faith in me at all. You remind me of the apostles. I was asleep in Peter's boat, and in panic they woke me up out of a deep sleep to tell me they were all going to drown. I was very annoyed, not only because they woke me up, but because they had no faith in me. In pictures you see me standing up in the boat, and calming the storm. Now, does that make sense? How could I stand up in a boat that was being tossed every which way? I merely grabbed the side of the boat and sat up, looked at the raging waters, and yelled out at the storm, 'Calm down,' which it did, and I just pushed myself back on the pillow and went back to sleep. See how simple is was for me to calm a raging storm! Whether the storm is in nature, or the storm is from the messes you make in your lives, I can calm them all just as easily, by a simple word. So, stop fretting and panicking! I am with you all the time and I am not going to allow anything to destroy you. Ask the Holy Spirit for trust. Your trust is so feeble."

What Is the Overriding Spirit of Our Life on Earth?

Jesus, what is the overriding spirit that you intended should pervade our lives here in this world?

"That you live your lives fully, not for yourselves, but in caring and beneficial relationships with one another, knowing all the time that I am part of your lives. I have given you all you need to live happy lives. I want more than anything that you be happy. That does not mean that there will not be sorrow and tragedy, because it is in those difficult times that you grow; grow to understand yourself and others, and that you can never find complete happiness in yourself or in anything in this world, but only by looking within and finding me within you. By preserving the childlike spirit that I gave you at birth you will never lose the sense of awe and wonder, which is the wellspring of knowledge and science and fills the soul with joy and exultation. Everything around you is a miracle of creation, and reflects the delicacy of my love for you.

"There are times when tragedy happens, and although that is painful, there are so many things that can be learned from pain and tragedy. Those experiences are necessary to draw you away from contemplation of material wonders into a contemplation of the emptiness of your life without me and how much you need to depend on me for strength and wisdom and the courage to endure the heavy crosses in your life. Those are the times when I draw you closest to me, because I know how frail and weak you really are, and that without my presence you would find it too difficult to cope. And it is during those times that you learn to have compassion and sympathy for others, whom you previously may have looked upon in a critical way as being weak or sinful. But by seeing your own frailty you learn not to judge others, but to understand them, and appreciate them, and in the process you learn humility, which has to be the only sound foundation of genuine holiness. "In living this way you will notice that there is within you a deep sense of peace, not the kind of peace that comes from being without troubles around you, but a peace that can come only from me, a peace deep within you, that comes from the realization of my presence with you, and your intimacy with me.

"That bond between us forges a warm partnership which allows me and the Holy Spirit to use you as an instrument of accomplishing wonderful things through you that benefit others and make your presence wherever you are a gift that continually enriches their lives and makes them realize that it is not you, but my presence within you, that is the source of something beautiful that touches them deeply.

"And that is what your life on earth is, very simply, nothing complicated, very simple and a joyful, even if it is sometimes a painful adventure."

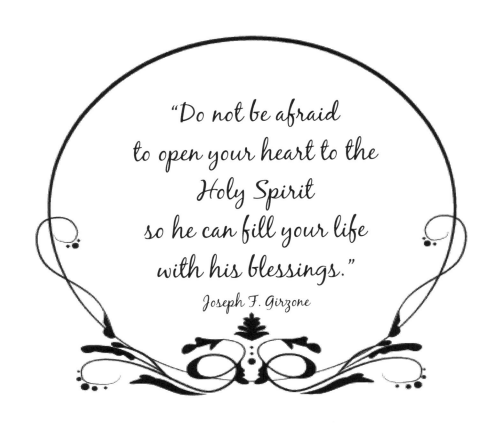

"Do not be afraid
to open your heart to the
Holy Spirit
so he can fill your life
with his blessings."

Joseph F. Girzone

Some Lives Are Smooth-Running Comedies
and Some Are Dramas

Jesus, why is it that it is impossible not to worry?

"Because you don't like drama in your life. You would like things to move along smoothly, so you can feel comfortable. But, some people live dangerously and they create turmoil and disturb the smooth course of their lives and send everybody into panic. Still, I tell you, 'Trust me!' I work just as well in dramas as I do in comedies. And in the last act there is always a happy ending. So, still I say to you, 'Stop worrying. There is nothing I can't handle, and I love you all too much to let anything happen to you."

The Inner Life of God

Jesus, tomorrow we celebrate the Feast of the Holy Trinity. That is a mystery which we will never be able to understand. Why did you jeopardize your life to reveal it to us?

"Because I wanted to be really close to you, and the best way I could do that was by revealing my inner life to you. It was important that you know that I am different. As my friends, you had to know the true identity of God. You may be made in the image of God, but the being of God is not that simple. You reflect God by your intelligence and will, your ability to think and to love. But in God, that is not all that God is. God is a living process of thinking and loving. What God thinks he gives life to, what God loves he gives existence to. So, you can see that I am the image come forth from my Father's mind, and the Holy Spirit is the living impulse of love that comes from the divine will possessed by my Father and me. We are each different, but we are inseparable. We think and love as one, but we each function on our own. I know you cannot understand that, but I had to share it with you, so you could in some way know that I would like for you to know who I am, even though you cannot fully understand me. It was just one beautiful way I could show you how much I love you, even though I died for revealing that to you.

"My Father created you, I died to save you, and the Holy Spirit makes me alive inside you."

"That bond between us forges a warm partnership which allows me and the Holy Spirit to use you as an instrument of accomplishing wonderful thing."

Joseph F. Girzone

111

God Trying to Partner with People

Jesus, if we were to ask you how you feel about our partnership relationship with you, what would you say to us?

"Most of you don't know how to partner with me. You know the right things to say to me, but you don't believe what you say. When you have a crisis or you run into difficulties, you pray for help, and I respond, but you ignore the hints and the suggestions I make clear to you, telling me in effect, they're not practical. You are struck by an unexpected happening in your life, which I thought would help you, but you pass over it, with a foolish comment like, 'Oh, wasn't that nice,' rather than say, 'I'll have to think about that and act on it.' There was a man in a deep crisis with an almost insurmountable problem who prayed to me for help. I responded to his prayer in record time and arranged for three strangers to 'accidentally' meet him. Each of those men was impressed when they met him, and had the means and the wisdom to solve his problem, and they were willing to help him. But he refused their help for different reasons: one, he didn't like his personality; the second one, he thought he was too overbearing; and, the third he didn't like because he was a Muslim. So, what could I do? This is a problem I have with so many. They don't know how to be a trusting partner. They pray, but they don't have faith in their prayers. It's like prayer is the thing to do, but you don't expect anything to come of it.

"You don't know how difficult it is for me to work with people. All they do is talk, but rarely listen, and if they don't listen how can I talk to them? And when I plop ideas right in front of them, and they don't think they are deserving of consideration, what more can I do? The bottom line is, they know how they would like to see their problems solved, and it has to be solved in their way. I know how the problem can be solved in a way that will have a much better result into the future. But, they are not ready for that, so they conveniently look upon those ideas as impractical. Unfortunately, they don't even consider that the ideas might have come from me, and might be worthwhile considering.

"So, there you have it in a few words. It's frustrating working with people. It reminds me of long ago, when people liked what I said but didn't really think it was practical. It will always be the same. And that is unfortunate, especially on an international level because their worn-out solutions end up destroying and damaging so many lives."

The Most Important Message to the World!

Jesus, what is the one thing you consider most important for our world today?

"The one thing that is essential for the survival of humanity is love. That is becoming rarer and rarer, and threatens to tear the world apart. People think nothing today of destroying others with whom they disagree. The news media thrives on exposing and destroying people. Members of political parties' delight in destroying their political opponents and their families. Competitors in business do all they can to destroy those who compete with them. Leaders of nations hold grudges over offences committed decades again and deem it cowardice and weakness to make peace with those who offended them. Sins against the poor are particularly odious because they come from slick versions of hatred and the worst kind of hatred—contempt. They secretly wish the poor would all die or just disappear. Even the thought of them is repulsive. Members of other religions are victims of an insidious kind of hatred because as it spreads it can eventually become the cause for civil wars and wars among groups of nations.

This is the greatest evil threatening the world today, and the one thing I consider not only important but critical is that you love everyone, and exclude no one from your love, not even evil people. They need love more than anyone and if you want to be my friend, you must love the way I love, and everyone you meet must see, not you, but me living in you and loving them through you. To do less is to not be faithful to me. And if you let my love reach out through you, one by one, others will learn to love. It is the only hope the world has for peace and harmony among nations."

Forgive, Always Forgive!

Jesus, how do we learn to forgive?

"Slowly. Forgiveness is not a virtue you acquire the first time you try. It is a gift you have to pray for continually, and when the Spirit decides to give you the grace to start, you will be able to take your first step. Up to that point all you can do is pray for the grace. But, when you are given the grace do not refuse it. If you accept the grace, you act on it and take whatever step you have the strength to take. It may be just a kind word to the person, or just a smile of recognition. Even that may not be easy, but it is at least a step which you do not have to express in words, which may be too difficult.

"To be able to express forgiveness may take a long time. Forgiveness is not easy. If you make a simple effort each time you see the person, and can make a simple kind gesture, it will help to make the pathway smoother, and lessen the tension and the stress you may feel. If you try to understand the person and learn something about the person, that often helps you to know why the person does things that are offensive. Often they have their own difficult personal problems and don't intend to hurt others, but just act out their discontent or other inner problems that are torturing them, not realizing that what they are saying or doing hurts others.

"The important thing about forgiveness is that it is never easy, but if you develop the habit of forgiveness, that habit eventually, over many years, becomes a normal way of acting. You eventually reach the point where you just assume the person is having a difficult problem and doesn't really intend to hurt anyone, and you aren't offended. Forgiveness is important because it is the key to true inner peace. That is why I was so uncompromising about my disciples making it a normal part of their life. I was not imposing on you an impossible burden. I just wanted you to have peace in your hearts, and radiate my holiness to others."

Though We May Experience Desolation, We Are Never Really Alone

Jesus, people often have the experience that the world around them is slipping away from them and they have the terrifying experience that they are alone on this planet. I once had that experience when I had taken my mother and father on vacation with me and we stopped in the middle of the Painted Desert in Arizona and walked through the huge petrified trees lying scattered all along the desert sands. I knew these trees were once alive hundreds of millions of year ago, but now all was total desolation. My parents had walked off into another area where they were out of sight, and I immediately sensed what it would be like to live on this planet with no one else in existence. The sensation was so terrifying and was having such a profound emotional effect on me that I had to distract myself. I found my parents analyzing a huge gorgeously colored tree trunk about forty feet long. We continued walking around and eventually left. Ever since that experience I could understand the panic people feel when they experience desperate loneliness. I think sometimes that was an experience I was supposed to have so I could understand other's pain of loneliness.

"Loneliness is one of the most devastating experiences a person can have. To do my work it is necessary to experience what they experience so you can understand. Without that experience people's pain and suffering would be a mystery. Books and lectures cannot take its place. When I came down to earth everything was a new experience for me. It had to be so I could learn everything about what you all feel and experience. I had come to earth to take upon myself the pain and burdens of all of you. So, I had to know from experience all that that meant. It was very painful, but it was the only way I could learn to understand your pain. At times I felt that loneliness as if I was on a planet all by myself, although there were thousands of people around me. I knew and understood everyone and the pain in each of their hearts, but I felt a dreadful loneliness in realizing that to all of those people I was a stranger and they never allowed themselves to be close to me. I never felt they loved me, they just needed me. At night when I went up into the hills to sleep, a terrible loneliness overwhelmed me. At times my Father let me absorb that loneliness when I couldn't reach out to him and feel the comfort of his presence. It was a small taste of the desolation I later experienced on the cross.

"When people share their experience of this loneliness, comfort them with the realization that during that experience I am closer to them than ever, because I know how dangerous that feeling is. Tell them to use that time placing themselves in my presence, and resting their head on my shoulders and let me hold them close, so that they can know they are not alone, and that I love them deeply. That painful time can be filled with special grace as I draw them closer to me, and help them realize that I am never far away from them.

But, that experience can also be dangerous, so they should distract themselves from it before it takes too deep a hold on them. It is only an emotion and the loneliness is only an illusion, but it is not healthy to entertain it. Teach them to distract themselves from it."

Never Underestimate the Power of Prayer

Jesus, how do our prayers affect those we pray for, even if they are strangers or are not nice people?

"I will tell you a story. A young boy heard the reader in church reading my words, 'If someone is mean to you, pray for that person.' Now this young boy was strong and liked to fight, but after he heard my words, he thought about them for the longest time, and told himself that he would never fight again. Now there were boys in his school who were bullies. They would take turns annoying and humiliating the young boy in front of others, especially girls. The young boy was sorely tempted to fight and knew he could hurt them, but he thought of my words that Sunday morning, so he just turned and walked away, even though the bully continued harassing him. The other bullies at different times treated him in the same humiliating way, yet he did nothing. He just continued to walk away.

"When he had walked far enough away, he began to cry, not because he was hurt, but because he was so angry and wanted so much to fight back. But, instead he did what he had heard me say that morning in church, 'Pray for those who are mean to you.' Now, when I saw the boy being so loyal to me and so brave, I wanted to help him and would have taught those other boys lessons that could have been painful, to protect the young boy, but I was so moved by the boy's prayers for the other boys, I changed my mind. Instead of teaching them painful lessons, I decided to touch those boys' lives in a way that would completely change them over time. The behavior of each one of them slowly changed. As they grew older, they became more serious. Eventually, one became a lawyer and took more than most lawyers' cases of troubled people, or people with could not afford a lawyer. Another young man became a principle of a school and started programs to teach and train students who were not bright in book learning but had talents rarely developed by schools. Another of the young men became a doctor who treated people with serious emotional and mental disorders. The last of the young men—who was deeply ashamed by his behavior towards the young man who never fought back—spent much of his life working in dangerous neighborhoods trying to change the lives of troubled young people. He ended touching the lives of many of those children who lived in unhappy homes.

"None of those things would have happened were it not for the sincerity of that young boy's prayers, which touched my heart so deeply I was moved to respond in an extraordinary way to reward him for his sincerity and goodness. So often people think I don't hear their prayers or if I do, I ignore them, or forget about them. What they don't realize is that there is never a prayer that is ignored or goes unanswered. Every one of your prayers are precious to me, and I answer them all, and the more the prayers come from your heart the way that boy's prayers came from his heart, the more blessed is the response. Never underestimate the power of your prayers!"

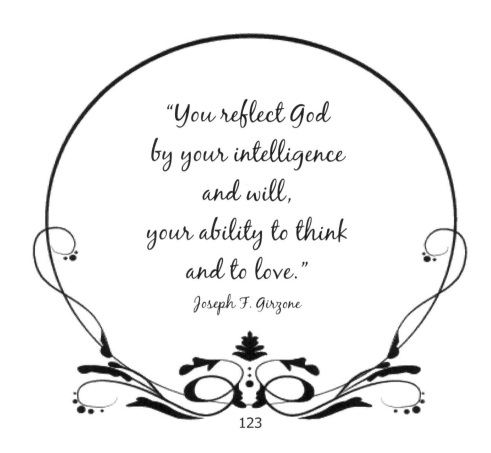

"You reflect God
by your intelligence
and will,
your ability to think
and to love."

Joseph F. Girzone

123

The Balance of Goodness in the World
Will Forever Increase, in Spite of Evil

Jesus, you are Goodness. It is the essence of your existence. How is it possible for you to tolerate evil, whether it is in the form of hatred or assault against your children, or damage to your creation?

"All evil is an attempt to do violence to me, even when it is directed against innocent people and against the poor. It is an assault against the divine majesty, and as such it is inspired by Satan's never-ending desire to increase the evil in this world. His ultimate goal is to create havoc and chaos among people in an attempt to destroy the balance between good and evil. His goal is to make evil triumph over goodness in a futile attempt to generate more evil than goodness in the world so he can boast of victory against me. Unfortunately, there are too many people who are fertile soil for the devil to sow his evil seed.

"When good people see this they become frightened and discouraged, but they should not be afraid. I have already conquered Satan and all his hosts of hateful followers. You saw little battles when you went places to talk about me, and plane flights were canceled, one airline going bankrupt just hours before your flight, and a man showed up out of nowhere to make new arrangements for you to assure your arrival at your destination. Just like world leaders strive to maintain a balance of power in danger spots around the world, so there is a struggle between God and Satan to maintain the balance between good and evil, and it is important for all good people to know that that balance of goodness will always be maintained and increased in spite of all the bad news that is displayed continually in the news.

"For every stroke of evil perpetrated against innocent and good people, holiness and heroism is increased among the victims even in the midst of their pain and intense suffering. Many witnessed this in the concentration camps during that horrible war. Satan's evil in the hearts of evil people is the seed of holiness and heroism in the victims, and the martyrs' suffering and death blesses the whole rest of my human family. So, never be afraid. Goodness is increasing steadily throughout the world, even though the news advertises mostly the sensational and the evil. They delight in the grains of dirt they find scattered at the bottom of the vast treasure chest of priceless diamonds, which is the goodness the Church spreads throughout the world. You have to trust that there is no way I will abandon my children, or my Church, which is my presence throughout history. You are too precious to me. Remember, I am still God and if I chose, I could destroy all evil at will, but my patience with evil human instruments stems from my love for them and my desire that they will one day repent and return to my love. That is the heart of the mystery of my divine love."

The Greatest Struggle Facing the World

Jesus, what is the reason for the great struggle in the world?

"It is simple. The two sides in the struggle are those obsessed with greed for power and money, and those concerned about the needs of the desperate poor. The needs of the poor are looked upon as the greatest obstacle to unbridled power and to unlimited accumulation of wealth. The needs of those obsessed with greed for power and money are the greatest enemy of the poor, denying that there are any sincere, authentic poor. The refusal to resolve that conflict will end up with a country controlled by a very small number of extremely wealthy and powerful people, and the masses of the citizens living in abject poverty and slavery. A balance can be reached only if the world wakes up to the fact that the talents and genius I have hidden in the poor, are the hidden treasures for the continued material and spiritual prosperity of the world. Refusal to recognize that reality will in the end result in the revolutions of the poor and the final destruction of a country or the world. I have placed the poor in the world to assure a balance between greed and justice, not charity and justice."

What Is Really Important in Life?

Jesus, is there any one thing that all of us should ask ourselves?

"People rarely ask themselves the right questions. They are concerned about personal needs and sell-esteem and self-importance, and about survival. But they rarely go much deeper than that. The one question that is important is, 'What do I really want out of life?'

"People may ask that question of themselves but few wait around for the answer. That is a basic question because it determines a person's automatic guidance system. Once a person asks that question and decides on that goal, the person's path through life is automatic after that, if that goal is taken seriously.

"But once a person asks that question, there are other related questions that follow, and these are the critical ones: 'Where will that goal take me at the end of my life? When I reach the end of my life what will be important to me then? If I find that something else may be important to me then, will I be prepared for that?'

"At that point the person might consider: Maybe I should make what will be important to me at the end of my life my real goal at the beginning of my life. If people were to take the time to ask themselves those questions, it would prove very fruitful."

"Anyone who tries to follow in
my footsteps
and live the way I live
will experience the same
rejection and ridicule."

Joseph F. Girzone

God Works Slowly, but Is Very Thorough

Jesus, how does the Holy Spirit work in the Church?

"Slowly. It took my Father till Abraham and Sarah were almost dead before he gave them an heir. It took him another five hundred years before he called Moses to lead the descendants of Israel out of slavery in Egypt, and then another fifteen hundred years before it was decided that I go to be their Savior. Still during all that time, the Holy Spirit was working through the prophets guiding and forming the people he had chosen to prepare for my coming.

"My Father is never hurried. He is very thorough and plans every detail with precision. It is the same with the Church. The Holy Spirit guides the present day apostles just as in the earliest days of my Church. It took almost three hundred years before he painstakingly led the bishops to a precise understanding of my identity as God and man. For each generation of bishops and theologians the Holy Spirit touches the minds of certain ones with new and surprising insights into what was previously known but only partially understood. They do not create new doctrines, but reveal new insights into truths already accepted and believed. This is in fulfillment of what I had promised the apostles, when I told them that the Holy Spirit would be their teacher and their guide, bringing back to their minds all that I had taught them, and would be with them until the end of time. During the past two thousand years the Church has grown in an ever-deepening understanding of me and my teachings, and has far surpassed what was known and written in the earliest days. That is part of the mystery of my Church. It is living, and because it is my mystical presence it is forever growing in depth of understanding of me and my Father and the Spirit, and of the needs of my earthly family.

Growth means change, and change is always necessary even though there will always be some who feel threatened by change. That is one reason why the Church moves so slowly, because there are so many who are slow and the Church is understanding of their loyal kind of piety. Nevertheless, there is never a need to hurry. My Father has all the time he needs to accomplish his plans with thoroughness. The Second Vatican Council is a good example. It is already fifty years since it produced all those wonderful teachings, but it will be more than a hundred and fifty years before people will appreciate them and they will become the accepted guide of the whole Church. Be patient. Don't look for rapid change, no matter how badly it is needed. We don't work that way."

Nothing Is Hopeless

Jesus, what hope can people with hopeless problems possibly have?

"The artist who did the art work for one of your books was suffering from a problem in her life that seeming had no hope of changing. As she worked on each painting, she sensed something was happening, and by the time she finished the last painting, the hopeless problem no longer existed. She could understand what had happened. The boy you visited in Florida who was hopelessly injured in a motorcycle accident and had severe brain damage which the doctors said was hopeless, and said there was little that could be done to save him. They had already removed a large piece of the cranium to relieve the pressure, and just expected him not to last for very long. His mother said she would never give up her prayers for his survival. Three weeks later when you visited him again he was sitting up, could move his legs, and was conscious. A few weeks later he was back to work. Even the doctors were shocked at his rapid recovery, and said there was no way they could explain it.

"The time you had taken your mother on vacation with you, and you were driving on that winding, two-lane mountain highway, and as you drove around a bend you saw a trailer truck coming at you in your lane, and there was no way to escape because of the guard rail. Remember, you said to your mother, "Mother, this is the end, I love you. Close your eyes." And your mother told you she loved you. When you opened your eyes the road was clear. When you looked in the rearview mirror the truck was behind you. That was something people would really call hopeless, but it shows that for me nothing is hopeless. It just means we make a little adjustment."

Don't Concentrate on Evil.
Nurture a Light-Hearted Spirit.

Jesus, it is hard to be happy with all the discontent and miserable things happening in the world, and in so many people's lives.

"Misery will always exist and it will always be widespread, but it is not good to concentrate on evil. The human soul cannot comprehend it or cope with it. It is not healthy, and you should not fill your mind with all the sadness and grief that is presented to you all day long. To fill your mind with these things is dangerous and unhealthy. There is nothing you can do to alleviate it, and to even change it in the slightest way. If you see something evil and you have the power to change it, do what you can to make things better. Few people have the resources and the circumstances to bring about wide changes in the world. Everybody has a responsibility to make their little contribution for change, but then be detached from it, because there is only a little that you can do. You are not God.

"Look around you and take time to notice the good things, things that caring people do for others, things in nature that are your natural remedies for sadness and depression, the funny things comedians dream up. Even though they often have difficult problems themselves, they have the special gift of reflecting my light-heartedness to lighten your spirits. Remember that nothing is so bad that I can't handle it. So, don't think you have to play God and do the impossible. And be patient with others who are not as blessed as you are. See good in everybody and don't waste time bemoaning the stupidity of unhealthy minds; they will always exist. Complaining about them won't make them go away. They are like mosquitoes.

Learn to trust me, while doing what you can, and stay detached from your problems. Don't go to sleep with them. While you sleep, I am working for you, and it is easier because you're not in my way. Nurture a light-hearted spirit; it's the fruit of your trust in me."

I Gave you the Key to Heal the World, But You Threw it Away

Jesus, why can't the intelligent people solve the frightening problems that we face all around us?

"Because they cherish personal and national illusions that are foreign to the vision of the reality I have given to all of you. If they cherish and pursue their illusions, they are dealing with fantasies and not reality. They refuse to see the world and the needs of people through my eyes, and through the vision I gave to them, so they will struggle endlessly and with no success. The key is simple. My people come first. Material treasures are no substitute for the human treasure in their midst. They are trying to create heaven in this world, but all they are doing is creating a version of hell. If they resent the poor and treat them as an obstacle to progress, they will forever generate chaos, and chaos is the essence of hell."

How God Views Our Form of Government

Jesus, as we celebrate our country's, and our own independence, I wonder how you look upon our form of government.

It is the only form of government that guarantees the freedom that my Father has given to all human beings, whatever their personal beliefs might be, or whatever their conscience judges honest, as long as those beliefs and judgments do not infringe on the freedom of others. Even those who honestly do not believe in my existence have a right not to be humiliated or harassed because of their non-belief. I have greater respect for people's freedom to believe or not to believe than you do. You are inclined to bully and shame people who do not believe. I respect their freedom not to believe. Them not believing often is part of my plan, as they struggle through their lives, like Saul before his conversion. Faith is a gift, and I give it to whom I will. If I should withhold that gift from some because I have plans inscrutable to your human minds that is not your business to question or to ridicule. I will reward them for following whatever lights I give them and it is not your business to be their judge. Just be happy I have given you the gift of faith, so practice it with humility, and respect the freedom of others. That is what is beautiful about your form of government. It most closely reflects my thinking, if properly understood. Unfortunately, there are many of you who are ignorant of the basic rights inherent in your constitution, and they trample crudely into areas that are sacred.

"And remember, your country and its laws are respected by my Father if you understand that the world is mine, not yours, and that my children of other countries have rights which must be respected as well as people whom you call citizens. If I send my starving children to your country for just work for their survival, they are not to be considered criminals and hunted down like animals. All children belong to me, so your form of government cannot supplant my rights as God, or you will pray a high price if you abuse the freedom your form of government holds so sacred."

Why Do People So Easily Become Disillusioned with God?

Jesus, so many people share with me their disillusionment when a loved one dies, especially if the person is a child, or an infant, or a person was special, which made the death unusually tragic. People often think it was your doing and they become disillusioned. Is each death something you have decided?

"When I designed the universe it was fashioned in such a way that it would unfold automatically, following the laws and energy forces inherent in it. Once I created human beings with free will that changed everything. As long as they were disciplined and lived reasonably, doing what was good and healthy for them, the normal order would have remained on a steady course of growth as all of nature unfolded. From that point on I rarely tampered with the natural course of events. Unfortunately, the more sophisticated humans became, the more they tampered with my creation, experimenting in things they thought they knew and understood, but the more they experimented the more damage they did to the natural process I had placed in creation, and the more haphazard influences disturbed what before was controlled by balanced forces. The most damaging is their tampering with human births. I had placed a balance in the numbers of male and female births depending upon the needs of the large communities at various times and during times of natural catastrophic events. You have destroyed that balance by making your own convenient preferences.

"Another area is in the tampering with the food supply. That has to be done, but it is not always done carefully, and creates dangerous imbalances across the world. And when it comes to what people eat, that troubles me because so much of the food is contaminated with substances that can be very unhealthy over time. I don't play games with my creation, so I don't interfere with your decisions. All I can do is try to influence people to eat what is healthy. This is so important to avoid all the dangers to your genetic heritage. Everything I created was done with absolute precision and forethought into the millions of years. You have disturbed that masterpiece in a few generations, thinking you are geniuses in discovering new things, not realizing the damage you are doing, even though there were some benefits that happened accidentally, many times I made little adjustments to prevent worse damage from taking place.

"When people die, often it is the result of some of these influences. Other deaths are the result of accidents, or accidental circumstances. It is not wise for me to step in and prevent what is taking place naturally just because people might be upset. Let us not reverse the order of things at that level. Remember, I am God and you are my creatures, and not the reverse. What I do expect of you, and have a right to expect, is that you have enough trust in my goodness and love for all of you that if someone dear to you or very special in some way, dies, that is not an evil for that person, but the most wonderful blessing that can happen to them. Coming to heaven to live with me and our heavenly family is the greatest gift I can give to anyone. No one's death is a tragedy. The tragedy is your grief. Learn to share the joy of your loved one I have taken home. Often if a person's death was my decision it is because I have seen nightmares ahead for that person if I allowed him or her to remain on earth.

"Trust me. I do nothing out of anger or retribution. I act only out of love and concern for all of you."

Why Does Jesus Say Imitating Him Will Make a Person an Outcast?

Jesus, why do you say that following you and thinking the way you think and loving what you love will make you an outcast?

"Open your eyes! Read the gospels again, and notice how many people I felt comfortable with. The apostles couldn't understand me. They were dense and difficult and so stuck in the old ways; they tolerated me because they saw I had power that impressed them, and were proud that I made them important. The people loved my healing miracles but thought my teaching was ridiculous and made no sense. How could I say the poor were blessed, and victims of injustice and contempt were fortunate? I know the apostles talked behind my back and complained to one another that my teachings were impractical, and they were scandalized I made so much of the hated tax collectors, and criticized the priests and Pharisees. They thought I was making a big mistake by favoring the poor, whom even they despised. They would have been happier if I cultivated the wealthy and the powerful, rather than criticizing them all the time. Peter even walked away from me one day when he boasted to me that he thought he could get himself to forgive seven times, and I told him that it had to be seventy times seven times. The conversation ended, and he walked away and went and complained to the others that I didn't make sense.

"And you ask me why I say it will be difficult for anyone who tries to imitate me. Think of what I just told you and you tell me. The answer is so clear. You will always be alone, as I was always alone. Who could I talk to personally who would agree with the way I think, and with whom I could share? Anyone who thinks the way I think will always be considered odd and out of touch with the life of real people. Why do you think I went up into the hills at night to pray? It was to get away from people. I felt so alone with them. The way I talked was like a foreign language to them and was stressful for me. I had to spend my nights with my Father to restore my sense of identity and be healed from the painful sense of rejection I felt from people who came to me only for my healings and because I entertained them.

"Anyone who tries to follow in my footsteps and live the way I live will experience the same rejection and ridicule. They will always be considered radicals and bleeding hearts and leftists and socialists by those who can't understand the heart of my teachings. There will be few people who will understand them. People may like them because they are good people who care for others, but deep down they will always consider them odd and out of touch with real life. And don't tell me you can't understand how alone that makes them feel, knowing they can't share their thoughts and dreams without being ridiculed and called names even by their friends and family. To be with friends and family and have to keep to yourself your real thoughts and dreams, and make only small talk will always be painful. I tell you this because if they treated me this way they will treat in the same way anyone who wants to be like me."

Be Patient! Change Is Coming in Its Time.

Jesus, how can we have any hope for much needed change in the Church and in society with so many people who resist change and consider an infallible church council invalid?

"Don't be so impatient. Moses had the same problem. When he led my people out of Egypt, the whole older generation was contaminated by their loyalty to the gods of Egypt and all the pagan customs. The younger generation also knew only what their parents taught them. Moses tried to teach them about the God of their fathers—Abraham, Isaac and Jacob—but whenever he come up to the mountain for me to give him instructions, the people reverted to their old ways and worshipped the gods of Egypt. Moses was beside himself trying to teach these stiff-necked people, who resisted him every step of the way.

"Why do you think I kept them in the desert for forty years when they could have made the trip to the Promised Land in less than two weeks? It was because I was not going to allow them into the Promised Land until the whole old generation of who resisted change died off, and their children died off as well or were washed clean of the old religion, so that only the youngest generation, and those who were loyal to my Father were left. Then a wholly new generation of people loyal to the God of their ancestors could enter the Promised Land and begin an entirely new life with my Father as their God, their only God, and they as his people.

"It is the same today. Those who refuse to accept the changes that are so necessary for the growth of the Church will die off soon, and the vast numbers of the people begging for healthy change will see the Church rising to new heights of glory. The Church will again be the vehicle for me to become the Light of World with a clear message of love and salvation that will unite people of all religions and lead the world to the peace I had always planned. Don't give up. Change is coming in its time."

Jesus, Teach Us How to Live

Jesus, would you tell us how we should live our lives?

"Live simply! Each of you was made special. Love who you are and don't try to be somebody else; that will mess up your life. I did not make a mistake when I designed you. You can accomplish great things if you love who and what you are and walk with me through life. I made you to be my friend, so I will always be with you. Be happy, even when life becomes difficult and painful. Do not become frightened during those difficult and painful times. That is when you grow in wisdom and understanding and in courage to face the future. And always know that I am there with you.

"Do the best you can with what gifts I have given to you. I do not expect you to always be perfect. You will fall many times and makes many mistakes, but that's all right. Just get up and carry on with humility and a contrite spirit. What is important is not the mistakes you make but the care and concern you have for others. I did not make you for yourself. I made you to be my heart and hands to reach out and be an instrument of my love and healing to others, so that others may receive from you what I may not have given to them. Always be aware of that privilege, and it will be to your honor and mine that others' lives and perhaps whole communities may be enriched by the blessings I have passed on to them through your love and your caring.

"Do not worry about the future. You will suffer many things but that will make you strong and understanding of others. If you remain close to me each day, the future will be blessed and your accomplishments will be multiplied so that your goodness will spread, as you allow me to reach out to many more lives. And at the end of your life, the world will be a better place because you have passed through there, and have allowed others to see my love for them by the way you treated them."

Are There Limits to God's Mercy and Forgiveness?

Jesus, what are the farthest limits of your mercy and forgiveness when faced with human wickedness?

"I have no illusions about the extent of humans' capability for evil. In all of human history there is no evil or compounded evil, even the worst evil conceived by the evilest hearts that surpasses my mercy to understand and when truly repented of, that I have not forgiven or would not forgive in the future. I know what is on your mind; the trial that has been on the television.

"I will tell you what is most difficult for me, and that is the hatred of the self-righteous crying out for the destruction of one they judge deserving of death. I am only too aware of the evil that many of them have committed. Their unjustified demands for the destruction of another whom they have judged guilty are so offensive. That is what tests my mercy when I consider my judgment of their evil hearts because I see no sign of mercy or forgiveness in them, and no admission or even recognition of the evil in their hearts. That was the sin of the scribes and Pharisees of ancient times when I was on earth. When they justify their own hatred and denial of mercy to others, they strip me of the one thing that makes my mercy and forgiveness possible, and that is their honest, humble admission of their hatred and contempt for others they consider sinners. As I said long ago, 'If you do not forgive others,

148

neither will your heavenly Father forgive you.'"

"The world
can only grow
when there is
love."

Joseph F. Girzone

It Is Sad When Fear Dominates
International Relationships

Jesus, what are people afraid of? The longer I live, the more I see how common fear is in people's hearts. What is it they are afraid of?

"People who live in fear have, in most cases, never experienced real love, even as infants. Without love they never learn to bond. They live in a world of strangers, never learning to trust anyone. It is sad because they feel alone, and with the unhealthy loneliness of those who feel unloved. The world is like an empty planet, where people are unrelated strangers who come in and out of their lives, and no matter how close they may be, they will always be strangers. It is like living on a planet all by yourself out in the middle of space, without any one to care for you or to love you. For a person like that life is frightening, and the threat of danger is only too much a part of their life.

"For people who live in fear, it is difficult for them to draw close to me because love and intimate friendship is rarely possible for them. If they could come close to me, and begin to trust me and love me, their fear would go away, because they would know I will never let anything happen to them. My love drives away fear. It is fear on the part of important world leaders that is

the cause of all the crises between countries. They live in fear of one another, fear of personal rejection and public shame and humiliation and fear of failure. When a leader comes along who is not afraid, people who live in fear get nervous because a person like that shows no fear of reaching out and striking up new relationships and getting other leaders to work together. That is threatening to people with fear. That is why most leaders are not like that. Most underneath are afraid of failure and are too timid to reach out and establish healthy relationships with other leaders. They depend on the illusion of power to intimidate others to watch out and send out messages like 'Don't tread on me,' and 'I know what you're up to, so watch out.' With that mentality peace and cooperation between peoples becomes impossible, and suspicion of one another poisons international relationships.

"It is unfortunate, but people who have not learned love are becoming more and more common. And even worse, it is reaching the point where many people are afraid to love. That is more threatening than nuclear power run amuck. The world can only grow when there is love. Love has to be the engine that drives the world if the world is to be healthy and prosperous. Teach the world to love. Never stop teaching that. Unless people learn to love they will never know what joy it is to love God, and experience the joy and intimacy of my love for them."

Faith Is Fragile and Must Be Nurtured

Jesus, does it concern you when people have doubts about matters of faith?

"People believe because I have told them about the things they believe. It is based on their confidence that I know what I am talking about. Believing in me and who I am is another matter. They believe in me and acknowledge me as the Son of God because they have decided to accept what I said I am based on what they have read about me in scripture. My life has touched them deeply, so they accept what has affected them so deeply.

"In time that belief in me and my teachings can grow cold and they may have forgotten the powerful effect I had upon them originally. That can happen for many reasons. Mostly it is because they fail to nourish their faith, or listen to others who believe differently and allow them to undermine their faith that has grown weak from not being nourished with good reading and consistently exercising their faith by prayer and conversing with others who believe, and by worshiping faithfully.

"Even people with strong faith may have doubts. That is natural because faith is not like mathematics. With mathematics, you can see it in front of you. If you put four objects on the table in front of you, and four more, you can see and count the eight. Matters of faith are not that certain. There can never be absolute certainty in matters of faith, so doubt can always occur, especially in times of emotional upheaval or depression. On the cross, I questioned my Father's concern and care for me. That came from pain and from the sight of my enemies humiliating me and heaping scorn on me, though deep down inside I knew my Father loved me.

"Because faith is fragile it is important to nourish your faith by reading and developing intimacy in your friendship with me. By being conscious of me in your life throughout each day, our relationship will grow stronger, and what was only faith in me, you have now experienced my real presence in your life and that supplants what before was just faith. Things that you have accepted on faith—like the Trinity and my presence in Communion and the reality of the divine life that comes to you in baptism—can at times become subject to doubt. Prayer alone can strengthen your faith in matters like that, knowing that I was the one who revealed those teachings to you."

When You Grow Old Your Best Work
May Still Be Ahead of You

Jesus, many of the people who call me or come to visit are elderly and are very concerned about dying. What am I to tell them?

"Age is a number. You should not become obsessed with age or with dying. It will strip the joy of living from your hearts, because you will think of all those you love whom you will leave behind, and they may need you. No one needs you. They need only me if I choose to work through you. I can still help them without you. To worry about leaving them is morbid and will kill your ability to dream of what you can still accomplish. When this happens you begin reliving the past with all its problems created by mistakes you made. Once you repent of past mistakes and bring peace to anyone you may have hurt, the past no longer exists. Don't ever think about it again.

And don't waste time thinking about the future; the future is not here. Only the present is real. Live for each moment and do your best with each moment, and on waking in the morning dream of the good things you can accomplish during that day. In that way you will be looking forward with enthusiasm for all the possible good things you can accomplish, not necessarily for yourself but for others, especially those whom you know would appreciate any little kindness you may do for them, as an expression of your love for me.

"And don't ever think you are too old and that you should be dead or might be dead soon. That is a total waste of time. I will not take you home until the work that I have designed for you to do is finished. If you are still on earth it is because there is still work for you to do, even if you are confined to bed or to wheelchair. The elderly has wisdom that is valuable; sharing it is a blessing to those who receive it and accept it. For those who are unable to do anything, it is their goodness that inspires others to see how beautiful life can be if they choose to live their life in my love. Even people confined day and night to a bed can be a powerful inspiration to those who know them, and live with them. The goodness that comes from holiness and intimacy with me radiates to other souls even though they may never do more than just lie in bed day and night. Holiness does not need external actions to inspire others. Holiness and beauty of soul is more brilliant than the light of the sun and its ability to heal and inspire is awesome.

"The soul who lives with me and in my presence, is in itself a ministry that makes my love and my presence real to others. Be content just to be, knowing that I am there just to be with you, and allowing others to see me through you."

What Children Need to Experience at Home

Jesus, how can parents best prepare their children for life?

"By loving them and placing their children before themselves. Children know when they are loved and when they are in their parents' way of being free to live their own life or follow a career. Parents have to be free to grow the way I made them, but not at the cost of their children feeling rejected or that they are in the way. To grow in a healthy way, they must know they are loved, and they must experience the love and caring and respect their parents have for each other. Children bond with their parents at a very young age, really in infancy, and they bond with the person they know loves them. Hopefully, it is not a babysitter or a childcare person. That bonding becomes the channel through which that child's thinking and attitudes and basic beliefs are molded for life.

"The parent is the natural teacher of a child. The bonding is what gives credibility to what is taught to a child. For that reason, there is no substitute for a parent teaching a child about God and faith and love and caring for others, and about the most important values in life. If that responsibility is left to strangers, even strangers who are religious, what is taught is like a skin graft. It is a foreign substance and is easily discarded. What parents teach their children about God, and love and caring and important values for life, will last because it is a natural part of their life together. It is the way life is lived at home and by the family. If that is not a part of a child's life experience, whatever a stranger teaches the child will mean nothing.

"It is critical that they be taught that they belong to God, who made them and loves them, and that he is a father, who cares for them with a mother's love and a father's love, strong and tender and always nearby to protect and heal.

"Even as infants, children should be taught respect for what belongs to others. That is the beginning of justice. Children should also be taught compassion and forgiveness because that is critical for them to know that as a child of God that is the way they should be towards others. Each child has been created special with a special purpose and a special work in life, and that the secret to happiness is in being close to me and allowing me to be a partner through life so we can work together, as I alone hold the key to the child's happiness and success."

"If a child is raised with these guiding thoughts, that child will grow happy and enjoy a special freedom knowing that I am his or her friend and am always there in happy times and troubled times."

Judgment of Others Is Always Based on Ignorance

Jesus, you once made a remark, "Do not judge and you will not be judged!" What brought that on?

"People make snap judgments about people when they don't even know what they are talking about. Each person's life is filled with complications and circumstances that are so intricately involved with plans I have not only for themselves but with plans involving many other lives that move in and out of the person's life. Things that happen which you might easily look upon as sins, and strange, bizarre behavior is none of your business. It is ridiculous for you to judge a person whose life I intentionally make impossible for you to understand because I needed that person's difficult behavior to make another person's life make sense and accomplish something very important. Sometimes I may allow things to happen which you may judge sinful, but that is not for you to judge. Something is sinful only if it is against my will, and if I need something to happen that you might judge evil to prepare a person for what I have planned for that person in the future, that's my business. When Moses accidentally killed that Egyptian soldier, that was not a good thing, but I allowed it because it was necessary for Moses to be humble and never to forget that he was a sinner when I later called him to be the great lawgiver of a whole civilization.

"People's lives are very complex and are intricately mingled in with happenings and occurrences that involve many other people. Each of you, even the most reticent, touch thousands of lives and without your even knowing it change the course of many people's lives by simple actions or gestures you may not even be aware of. I am very involved in each of your lives. That is why the life of each one of you is necessary to me because I made you and planned your lives in such a way that you are, without even realizing it, related to one another and affect each other's lives.

"So for you or any of you to make quick judgments about anything any of you do is out of line because you really don't know what you're talking about. Another person's life is like the back of a tapestry for you, and it will never make sense. My mind is like the other side of the tapestry as I weave the tiny details of everyone's involvement with each other so that when they thread all your lives are finally in place the result is a masterpiece. When you finally see that then you will know how ignorant it was to be so judgmental."

The Honest Recognition of Our Nothingness
Is the beginning of Holiness

Jesus, what trait in us do you find most attractive?

"The humility of a person who finally realizes that he or she is a sinner: That is so beautiful to me. It is more important than anything else, because it is the beginning of truth. That trait is like the perfume of a Night Blooming Cereus, and just as breathtaking as its flower.

"You may ask why that trait is so important. The answer is simple; because it is the only attitude that prepares a person to open their soul to me. You would be surprised how few people have arrived at that recognition. Remember many years ago when you gave a talk downstate, and you mentioned in passing that we all make mistakes and fall and that we are all sinners. A lady spoke up, deeply offended, and said, "I am not a sinner." It is rare to find people who have really learned to face the reality of themselves and can honestly feel that they have sinned and have hurt others and have been offensive to me. So many people treat me as if I was an equal to them. With that kind of arrogance, the door of their hearts is locked tight against me. They feel no need for me, and try their best to get along in their lives without me. And I never force myself into a person's life. I am just there waiting patiently for them to reach a point when their life or their health or their family is threatened and they feel helpless. They then cry out in desperation for me to help them. But, that doesn't last long. Once the crisis passes, they walk away without even saying thank you.

"So, when someone sincerely expresses the awareness of their sinfulness, it touches my heart deeply, because the person has finally come to the realization of just what they are: weak, frail humans who are helpless without my strength and my love, and my presence within them that gives them a life that is real and not a self-created pretense. When a person like that looks up to me, the look alone says, 'Lord, I have nothing. Whatever I do have you gave me. Without you I am lost in a world that has no meaning. Help me.'

"People in the programs to fight addictions have arrived at that point in their spiritual life. They are honest people who have finally realized the emptiness and frailness of their humanity and their souls cry out for my love and my strength, because they realize that alone they are helpless. They may not realize it, and others may not realize it, but they are beautiful in my eyes because they see their true selves as I see them. It is then possible for me to work miracles within them. And in their humble evaluation of themselves they are always there for one another, just like I taught my disciples originally, to always be there for one another."

Start My Fire Across the Earth

Jesus, how can we kindle that fire you wanted so much to spread throughout the world?

"Very simply. Refuse to hate, refuse to nurse evil thoughts about others, refuse to spread gossip and evil things about others, and always look for the good in others, even if it is hard to find.

"In short, learn to love others the way I love you. None of you are very lovable by my standards, but I still love you even though you have nothing to offer. So, all I ask is that you have a little decency to show that same gracious love that I show you. Treat others that way and it will be like a spark on a dry grassy meadow in the burning heat of the Son."

Faith Is Not a Warm, Pious Feeling

Jesus, what is faith? I ask this because many people become nervous when they lose their nice warm, pious feeling when they pray. They then think they are losing their faith.

"Faith is not a feeling. Faith is an untiring and tenacious clinging to me. It is like a compass and is an unwavering focus on me which nothing can push off course. When that nice feeling of piety wears off and you still pray and think of me, that's faith. When you do what you know is right even though you feel like doing something evil, that's faith. When you go to church and pray and you feel nothing inside but distractions and emptiness, but still kneel there deaf and dumb, that's faith. When you do good things for others and you get abuse for your reward, by continuing to do doing good things, that's faith. When you are treated shabbily or unkindly by a priest or minister, yet still go to church, that's faith. When you try to be kind to desperate people needing help and are ridiculed by other Christians, yet you still continue your good deed, that's faith. When your priest or minister turns you away when you need help or you offer to be of help in your parish, and you still go to church even though you feel unwanted, that's faith. When bishops or leaders in your church treat you with contempt and disdain and you still treat them with respect and remain loyal, that's faith. When with all your best efforts to do what you think is right and you fail, yet still maintain your focus on me, that's faith. When you lose all, you have and are reduced to inner emptiness as well, and your focus on me is still clear and unchanged, that's faith. When you see other Christians, even priests, and other clergy doing evil things, and in spite of the hurt and disillusionment it causes you in your respect for them, you still remain loyal to your religion and its beliefs, that's faith. When you are in ill health, and pummeled by changing conditions in your life and need the help of fellow Christians, especially clergy, and no one is there for you, yet you still love your religion and cling to me, and do not become bitter, that's faith. When one by one loved one's die, and friends drift away and you realize that you are alone on this earth, yet your love of your religion and your clinging to me is still as strong as ever, that's faith. In the end we still have each other. That's all that matters."

Church Is Supposed to Be Family, Not an Institution

Jesus, don't you think that keeping faith in the Church is a bit much when there are so many things attached to church that are offensive, like arrogant, pompous bishops and priests and people rigidly obsessed with the legality of issues, rather than compassion for people.

"I told the apostles to go out and convert the world. They did and are still doing it. Now my family is huge, embracing the whole world. People make a mistake when they call it an institution. It is my family, and it is composed of many thousands of small families. That is the only part of church—the small neighborhood family—that affects individuals like you and others. Those families may be considerable in numbers, but if you all had your hearts in the right place, you would adjust your thinking and look upon your parish as family. But, you are the problem. You don't want to be part of family. You all want to be independent. You want to choose a few friends and ignore everybody else. Remember, many years ago, when you were first ordained, and you worked in The Bronx. Your parish was large, you had your own low school and high school, and all your people lived in a rather small area, with very large apartment houses, where two and three hundred families lived. They came to church on Sundays and went back home and locked their doors and many never got to know people who lived in their own apartment building. People choose their own privacy and isolation from others, and want to choose just a handful of people to be friends. That is not what I had I mind when I created my Church. I wanted it to be family where everyone knew one another and cared for one another. When you choose privacy and isolation from others, rather than reaching out and embracing members of my family, you give it the appearance of an institution, and then when you are hurting and you reach out to others for help, no one knows you because you made yourself a stranger. You then resent being treated like a stranger and you start calling the Church names. That is what happens when so many of you choose to be strangers and you turn your church into an institution. Since so many of you chose to live isolated from the others you prevent my Church from being family, and it then acts like an institution. Yes, it is hard to keep faith when you have done this to my family. When you start finding fault, maybe you should look inside yourself and see if you have not contributed to what your local family has become. If it is dysfunctional, maybe you have contributed to that dysfunction.

"Bishops and priests are no different than the chief priests and leaders in my own day. Many are good and caring and many are obsessed with customs and traditional practices, and are obnoxious. And they too create problems, and contribute to the dysfunction in my family. But, if everybody worked more closely together and exerted more influence on one another. Make friends with your clergy, whether they want to be friends or not, and in this way you can break them down and make them more human, and many of those problems could be taken care of. But people choose not to speak out and make their influence felt until it is too late. And then all you do is complain. Become involved! Be part of the family and speak out with other members of the family and make your family what it should be. That's what I did when I was down there years ago. My local leaders were obnoxious but I still made my presence and my influence felt. I spoke out continually. Unfortunately, like today, most people don't. They would rather just walk away and complain."

What Does Jesus Expect of Us?

Jesus, what is it that you expect of us?

"Not much. I recognize that you have very little to offer, so I don't expect very much. In reality, the most you can give is a heart open to accept what I have to offer you, so that you can be a willing and supple instrument of my love and caring for others.

"Don't overestimate your importance. Your importance does not come from what you have to offer me but what I have to offer you, if and when you let me. Your importance is limited only to your free acceptance of me into your life. If you allow that to happen, then a wonderful adventure can begin with the two of us as partners. But, you must give me the freedom to work through you and I never lose a chance to do that with people. It's our partnership that is important, and the intimacy that that partnership entails. As we get to know each other, our friendship and intimacy grows. As our intimacy grows others see me in you and in others who let me into their life. It is all very simple; when we work together, I can use you to touch other people's lives in ways that you would never imagine. And that's what it is all about."

How Should We Treat Sinners?

Jesus, how should we treat sinners, and people who have done evil?

"The same way I treat you. Think about that."

The Cure for Our Country's Ills

Jesus, what is happening in our country and throughout the world is depressing. It seems no one has the intelligence to even understand the enormity of the problems or what is necessary to solve them.

"Stop worrying. Hard times are necessary to bring people back to reality. Times of great prosperity generate decadence and rampant immorality. Sports become violent to satisfy people's jaded craving for excitement. Worship fades when people become addicted to money and no longer feel the need for God. Children feel they are in the way of their parents' freedom. Everybody suffers when material prosperity replaces me. Christians may mouth my name in an expression of false patriotism, but their real love is obsession with money. That is the problem with your political life. The struggle is between the needs of the poor and greed for money, and it is Christians' obsession with money that is destroying your economy. Only mining the talents and genius of the poor will revive the stagnation of your country's growth as a world leader. Trust in money has replaced trust in God, and you fail to see the dormant richness I have hidden in the poor. When you take seriously what I said continually about the poor, you will have found the key to true prosperity. When you demean the poor, and favor the rich, you will soon end with a country run by a handful of extremely wealthy people and the whole rest of the country will be poor peasants. Unless you all wake up, that will take place in less than fifty years.

"If people have a change of heart, come back to me, and take my teachings seriously, I will make whatever adjustments are necessary to reset your country on a path to growth. I know human leaders cannot do it. They don't even understand the problem. Look how they are fighting now. When Christians take me seriously, I will heal your wounds. For me it just takes a little adjustment to set things right."

How to Stop Worrying

Jesus, do you have any advice as to how we can start each day without worrying about a whole list of unresolved issues?

"Yes. As soon as you wake and say your prayers, make a commitment to me that you will place all your concerns in my hands, and mean what you say, and say it with real trust in me, then go about your day tackling one problem at a time, without worrying about all the others. If you start to worry, banish the thought by becoming involved in something else, or tackling another problem, but don't let worry enter your mind. Keep your mind distracted from your problems and worries. In not too long a time you will have acquired the habit of not worrying. In this way your trust in me will grow, and you will worry a lot less."

What Is the Purpose of the Poor?

Jesus, I have a very difficult time understanding the whole debate about the poor. Some say there are no real poor. They say that if people are poor it is because they are just too lazy to work, and enjoy being taken care of by the government. Some say that most of the poor are not poor by choice but by circumstances beyond their control, and have to be cared for, either by government or churches or private groups who provide care. Jesus, why are there so many poor? And what is their purpose?

"I placed the poor in the midst of every society. It was not a mistake; it is not an accident of circumstances. The poor are the conscience of society. Their purpose is to make possible the salvation of those whom I have blessed with an abundance of gifts and talents and wealth. The reason why there is a debate and such anger over the poor is that their very existence bothers the conscience of the rest of society. When people acquire wealth they want to keep it. I never intended wealth to be kept but to be shared, to be a benefit to those I have given less, and to benefit the community and the country. What I intended to be a beautiful Christian virtue they debase by calling it evil, socialism. All wealth is mine. All talents and gifts come from me. I determine how my blessings to people should be used, and I never intended they should have hoarded by greedy people. They will pay a price for that one day.

"I intended that the poor be the means of salvation to the gifted. When a society finally recognizes the treasure of talent and genius hidden in the vast poor in a country, that society will then find the key to unimaginable prosperity. Otherwise, it will just be a matter of time before the society slides inevitably into decay—morally and economically. What pains me most is that people with little or no faith appreciate the poor more than most of those who call themselves my disciples, who resent the poor and hoard the blessings I have given to them. They don't mind giving token donations to the poor and starving and migrants far away, but they can't stand them in their midst."

The Carefree Spirit of Children

Jesus, what is it that you want most for us today?

"The carefree spirit of childhood. You all walk around as it there is a heavy weight bearing down on you. That is something I never wanted for you. I came to bring you freedom, but you managed to lose that freedom. When I told the apostles that they should become as little children, they had no idea what I was talking about. What I was talking about was something they had all lost, the simplicity, the trust, the innocence and the carefree joy of little children.

"None of you understand me. You think I enjoy putting heavy moral burdens on you, and holding you responsible for mistakes you make. That is the farthest from my mind. I want you all to be free and happy and unfettered from burdens. All I expect is that you care for one another. You can still be serious and fulfill your responsibilities without being weighed down by worry and anxiety. Most of you never even take the time each day to notice all the beauty and wonder in my creation all around you. You are always on that high-speed train that flies past all the magnificent sights and real life creations I display to you all day long, and they are nothing more than a blur to you because you are imprisoned in your anxieties.

"Life can be difficult and can have problems, but that does not mean that that you have to be obsessed with them day and night. Life's problems should not trouble you any more than a mathematics problem that you had in school. You don't live with it. You think about it and then put it aside and get on with the day. If it is a serious problem that demands attention, I am with you all day long, and all you have to do is share it with me. Your problem is that you don't believe I can do anything about it, as if I am not really real, but only a fantasy. I am real and I am God, and I can do anything, so why do you worry all day long when I am right there to help you. Get with it. I am there to help. There's no problem we can't solve together. Realize how lucky you are!"

How Do the Intellectually Handicapped Survive?

Jesus, there are tens of millions of people who do not have the mental capability to care for themselves. When their parents die, and their brothers and sisters don't want to be bothered with them, how do they survive?

"That's my secret. Remember I know each one of them and each one is special to me, even though they may be considered a nuisance to nice society. They are the troubled and crippled sheep in my flock and I watch over each one of them day and night. I often touch the hearts of decent people and arrange for them to meet those who need help, and there are many who cooperate with me. There are some who find shelters, and kind people along the way, and they are helped in really difficult situations. Sometimes they live in YMCA residences and other places like that, so they are protected from bad weather and have food.

"Each situation is unique, but I wander through the world day and night looking out for each one of them, as they are unwanted by society and are a nuisance to politicians. Someday a caring Christian, or maybe even one who has no faith, may respond to my grace and design little villages here and there, with cottages where small groups of them can live like little families, with caring people watching over them. There are already in many places

177

houses where small groups of them live and are protected. They are free to come and go, and they are provided for, but there are still many who seem lost. Occasionally, I arrange to take some home when their situations become too difficult for them. But, don't worry, I watch over each one of them, and when they come home with me, they will have places here in heaven that will be the reverse of what they had down on earth when so many of them were unwanted, and they walked through life lonely and forlorn. I am still the Good Shepherd and there is not one of my sheep that I do not watch over and care for."

The Importance of a Happy Spirit

Jesus, what is important for us all to develop within ourselves to preserve a free and happy spirit?

"It is important that you experience a quiet underlying sense of serenity and joy as you move through each day. Do not allow yourself to concentrate on problems and depressing matters that you can do nothing about, as that will only disturb the inner peace that you need to work through your responsibilities of the day with serenity. News, especially television news, is no longer news, but daytime theatre that presents carefully planned drama based on conflicts to capture your attention. This preys on your fears and insecurity and undermines a healthy, peaceful and happy spirituality that is necessary to maintain your confidence and trust in my love and protection, and irresponsibly manipulates your moods in a way that is dangerous. It is important spiritually that you maintain a calm and peaceful spirit and not let your inner life be controlled by others.

"The greatest gift I have given to you is your freedom. Do not give that freedom, especially that freedom of spirit, to anyone else's control. Respect and enjoy your freedom, and your happy spirit. No one can take that joy and happy spirit from you. You have to give it up, or let someone else control it.

179

Never let anyone take away your peace and happiness. That is my gift to you. Unhappy people may try to take that peace and joy from you because they themselves are unhappy, but only you can let them. Never let anyone control that gift that is so important for your happiness. If you do you will turn your life into a joyless and heavy burden.

"Be happy and never give up your happy spirit for anyone."

A Good Example of How the Good Shepherd Works Today

Jesus, I experienced today what you shared with us two days ago about caring for those tens of millions who have little to hope for in life.

I talked with a remarkable lady, now in her seventies, who lost her mother and father as an infant and grew up without a mother and father, totally alone in life except for some kind relatives who cared for her for a while. As she got older she married a man who was extremely abusive, and the relationship ended. She later married a man who loved her and was kind to her, and they helped each other to grow spiritually.

Touched by your grace, Jesus, the woman always had a kind spot in her heart for women in abusive relationships, and who had little or no hope for escape. Together with her husband's help, she passed the word around among friends that she would like to help any women in such difficult circumstances. A woman showed up one day with her child and this kind lady helped her find a place to live, and with friends' help she was able to get a crib, and diapers and blankets and other things the woman needed. Shortly later another woman came for help and this lady helped her as well.

A few days later this lady, I'll call her Pat, thought it would be nice if she started a shelter for these women to come to when they needed to escape dangerous situations. Gradually, the program touched the lives of more and more hurting mothers and their children as the days and weeks and months passed. In time, even though she had meager resources herself, Pat was able to find shelter and a new life for over a thousand mothers and their children. Then one day recently her husband died. It was a devastating blow and broke her heart, but still she would not give up.

Somehow she still managed to run her program and is still reaching out and helping battered and abused mothers. They come to her for help daily, and this gentle and no-longer young lady still works many hours each day to aid troubled and hurting mothers.

Jesus, I was so happy to meet this woman, as she is a good example of how you as Good Shepherd still reach out to people with no parents or loved ones and take them into your care and guide their lives one by one to a life that is peaceful and enriching, not just for themselves but for many others besides.

Thank you, Jesus, for sharing this woman's beautiful life with me so I could understand how intimately you enter the lives of the lonely and abandoned and be both mother and father to them, and use them as instruments to help you reach out to others who are alone and hurting.

Ingredients for a Happy Future

Jesus, what will be necessary for the healthy future of our country?

"Equal justice, abandonment of self-centeredness, caring for those in need, and development of the talents and gifts I have given to so many of your people for the creation of new ideas."

How to Face Difficult Problems

Jesus, so many people come with problems and are overcome with anxiety because they don't know how to solve them.

"The ability to solve problems has to be taught in childhood. Anxiety and panic does nothing. When a person faces a difficult problem the first thing to do is be calm, go to a quiet space, sit down, place yourself in my presence or in the presence of the Holy Spirit, and know that we are there. Then calmly open your mind and your heart to us for guidance. Share with us your problem and then sit back and meditate. Meditating with us is the most healing and fruitful kind of meditation, because you are calling on the power of God to guide you and help calm your spirit.

"As you meditate and face the problem honestly, ask yourself how the problem came about, and what are the causes. Are there any steps available to begin resolving the problem? If not, ask us for guidance. You will not hear voices and will not get a verbal answer, but be patient, and stay calm.

"As you meditate, you will notice that there are things you can do, maybe not to solve the problem, but to reduce it in a way that makes it easier to manage. Then, develop a plan, and take steps to reduce the effects of the problem, and see if you can find ways to work out part of the problem. Often a problem can be reduced enough for you to handle it until you can gradually find ways to work it out completely.

"Often when you pray, the next morning when you wake up, you find that you have a solution, or sometimes the problem disappears in a way you can't understand. A little adjustment was made while you were asleep.

"If a problem is of a kind you don't have the resources to manage, then find a friend or a person who can counsel you, and ask their help. Many problems you can resolve in these different ways. Some problems you just have to make up your mind to just walk away from them, unless they are loved ones, then just distance yourself from them emotionally, so you can find peace. Some problems are to help you to grow and will remain with you. Be patient; you can learn from them and they can make you strong and wise. But always know I will be with you in all your problems."

How Jesus Wants Us to See Him

Jesus, how do you want people to see you, Christ the King, The Ruler of the Universe, the Majestic God we worship in liturgy, or the simple, humble homeless wanderer in the Gospels, wearing a soiled robe, and tousled hair, and in the company of simple sinners?

"You are the ones who like to give me titles, but titles mean nothing to me, and it does nothing for you spiritually except push me back into eternity and distance me from you. The way I lived is the way I want all of you to remember me, the humble shepherd wandering daily with his flock of poor simple people. I know you are not happy with that image and it is you all who insist on looking on me as the Divine Majesty, and the King of the Universe. You mean well but I find that offensive. I chose to be poor, but the poor are obnoxious to you, so you resent me identifying with them, but that is what I have chosen. So, don't try to make of me an image I chose not to be. You are only destroying what I tried to be among you, your friend, a humble God living among you and sharing your life with you every moment and every day of your life, sharing your simple joys, and your dreams, and your pain and feelings of failure. I want only to be a part of each of your lives. So don't make me a God in your own image or you will push me away from you, and destroy your ability to become a friend to me."

What Is Prayer?

Jesus, how should we pray to you?

"Pray like you were talking to a friend. Know that I am with you always, and try during the day to be conscious of my presence. Then talk to me, or just think of me. Just knowing that I am there is a prayer. Recognizing who you are and who I am is a good start. You don't have to always say nice things and shower me with all kinds of flattery that you consider worship and praise of a divine being. I don't need nor particularly enjoy that kind of stuff. I know people say it because they think I like it.

"Just be aware of my closeness to you, and sharing your friendship with me is the best kind of honor and the kind that has meaning for me. It is sharing your heart with me sometimes joyfully, sometimes sadly, sometimes angrily, and sometimes depressingly. That kind of prayer has meaning because it is a real expression of what you are at those times, and I like it because you are being real with me. When you're angry, that doesn't bother me or offend me. It's just the way you feel and is an honest expression of something that is troubling you. I listen when you rant and rave. It's only noise. Sometimes I laugh, because it's often funny. I just wait until you get tired and calm down. Then you feel embarrassed, and if you are willing to listen, I sometimes make a suggestion, though most of the time you just needed to make noise."

"I like it best when you just keep your mouth shut and just be. Then you are able to listen. I share and you don't even know it. Later on, what I shared dawns on you and you think you thought it up yourself, but you really suspect it may be from me, because that is not the way you ordinarily think. What I like most is when you ask for help for others. Then I really listen, even though I may not answer in the way you like. I do know better what the person really needs, and I take care of that.

"Prayer should be simple; just a thought every now and then to let me know you're thinking of me, and it's nice when you make whatever you're doing an expression of appreciation for our friendship, and recognition of my love for you. Then I feel closest to you.

"Just knowing that you are my friend and I am your friend is what is important. I want nothing more."

What Is God's Idea of Justice?

Jesus, what is justice in your way of thinking?

"Justice is the recognition that every human being has rights that I have given to them and which no government has any authority to deny or strip from them. Among those rights are the right to be free and to worship God according to the rights I have given them: the right to work and earn what is necessary to live with dignity; the rights of those unable to work or care for themselves to be cared for so they can live with dignity; and the right to be treated and respected with equality whether the persons are wealthy or poor. With those rights is the responsibility of government to make sure that there are no members of society, whether citizens or refugees from degrading human conditions, who are forced to live in shame or degradation, or abandoned when in dire need. And there is no society that is exempt from these obligations, and no society should dare to call itself Christian if those rights are not honored."

To Know Jesus Is the Work of a Lifetime, and Few Ever Begin that Journey

Jesus, what is important as we get to know you?

"To understand how I think. If you do not understand how I think there is no way you can follow my ways. Too many of my disciples assume that the way they think is the way I think, and that the values and prejudices they have are the values that I have, so they see little in their lives that has to be changed. That is the problem with so many religious leaders; they assume that their own attitudes about religion and about religious practices and customs are the same as mine, when they are merely attachments to childhood memories. As brilliant as they may be, they have not grown spiritually because they never really took the time to become intimate with me so they could learn to know me. They kept intact things they were taught in childhood, and even though they may have studied extensively, they learned very little about me. Theological concepts are not the substance of the divine intelligence. They are the conclusions of theologians. That was the mistake the scribes and Pharisees made; they assumed that their religious ideas and teachings reflected my Father's mind. That was the problem then and it is often the problem today. So many religious leaders fashion God in their own image and impose their own 'divine' beliefs on what they demand of the people."

"That is why learning how I think and how I view so many thousands of issues and relationships is critical to being a mature and authentic disciple. There are very few who take the time to draw close to me and contemplate my life and try to get inside my mind and my heart. That is the process that must be followed every day of a person's life if they really want to know me and how I think and how I feel. It is not something people pick up out of the air. There are very few who really know me, and it is unfortunate that there is hardly any place on earth where people can go to learn about me in any depth. Too many just assume they already know me, and that there is little more they can learn about me that they don't already know."

The Parable of the Concrete Tomb

Jesus, what is the explanation of that horribly depressing experience I had earlier tonight when I saw so many people standing and being sucked into a wall of concrete. Some were almost totally encased, others were only partially encased, and some the whole front of their bodies from head to toe was visible but the back half of their body was already encased? The experience was so depressing, it made me feel as if my whole ministry to make you better known was futile, and I felt like giving up. Why did I take it personally? What did the message mean and is there something I should learn from it?

"The wall is faithlessness. It is like a concrete tomb. Persons encased in the wall are in varying stages of unbelief. Those who are almost fully entombed are those whose sense of superiority looks contemptuously on faith, which makes it very difficult for my grace to give them life. Those who are partially entombed are those Christians who profess to believe but reject much of what the apostles taught and what the earliest Christians believed. Many clergies who believe much of what I have taught, are still stuck on the trappings of their religion and resemble important worldly people. They refuse to be servants in my family, and look upon themselves as more important and superior to others. Their arrogance turns so many sheep and even other shepherds away from me.

"The message for you is that whatever others may be like that is not your business. It is your business to do your work and stop trying to be the messiah."

Touched by God's Grace

Jesus, will we ever wake up to the real crisis we face today and which so many people fail to see? Why can't we see it? It is so obvious.

"You choose to be blind and are bringing upon yourselves destruction worse than war. Tell the story of your friend who used to be very wealthy."

I have a friend. Years ago, he and his wife invited Sister Dorothy and me to Switzerland to talk to a group of their rich friends. We went and stayed at their chateau. The next day we spoke to a crowd of over a hundred and fifty people, many of them atheists. We spoke about Jesus. One of the persons in the audience was the Swedish ambassador to Switzerland, and Undersecretary-General of the United Nations. A Jewish lady played the hymns about Jesus on her keyboard, as the whole unusual group sang along, though they had never heard the hymns until that day. It was a wonderfully happy event. Afterwards, as I walked through the crowd still sitting as they talked to their friends, a man grabbed my arm. I looked down and saw it was the Swedish ambassador. He looked up at me with tears in his eyes and said, "Thank you, Father, thank you so much." I smiled and thanked him for coming.

That talk we gave was just a simple talk about the real flesh and blood Jesus the Jewish people saw centuries ago when he came walking down the streets in their villages. Most of the people there had never heard a talk about Jesus before, and the response was the same as the ambassador's.

Not long afterwards, the friends who had invited us and arranged for the talk, left Switzerland and come back to the United States where they built a mansion for themselves in Florida. The Jewish lady and her husband also came to the States and became Christians. Not long afterwards, my friends decided to move to Alabama and built another house there, but then the economy changed and they lost all their wealth when their vast investments collapsed. Without a job and no income, they had all to do to keep their house. Badly needing a job, the only one he could find was as director of a shelter and kitchen for the homeless and the poor, where he has been working ever since.

When I talked to him recently, I expressed how badly I felt for him. He told me that he had never been happier than he was working with the poor, who he found to be beautiful people. I told him I had a hard time understanding why so many people looked down on the poor and he told me something that shocked me, "I can understand how they feel. I used to feel that way. It's not because we are ignorant. It's because we choose to be blind and block their desperation out of our hearts for fear we may have to share with them. I have found what a joy it is to care for these people. They are beautiful. I have never been happier."

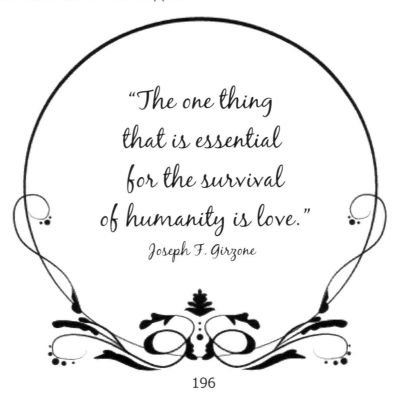

"The one thing that is essential for the survival of humanity is love."

Joseph F. Girzone

The Compassionate Heart of God

Jesus, there are so many things happening in the world today. What concerns you most?

"The starving millions of babies and how elected officials can see those babies and not show concern. What troubles me is that they can so easily block concern out of their hearts and go away and do nothing. 'Come to me... Depart from me... When I was hungry you watched me starve and did nothing.'

"And I am concerned about the elderly all around the world. Not long ago, many were important people and affected their communities in important ways. Now they are just 'that old man' or 'that old lady' that 'we see walking down the street.' Few know them anymore. They are just the faceless strangers who shuffle along as they walk alone, seemingly to no destination, or when seen in supermarkets reading with dimmed vision labels on packages to see what they are able to eat or can afford to buy. Their needs are few and their income is little, so many have to decide whether they will buy food or live in a cheap apartment, since they cannot afford both. It pains me that politicians want to shrink even more what little they have to live on rather than inconvenience the wealthy.

"What do you expect me to be concerned about? I am a happy God and joy is of my essence that flows from my love, but I am not blind. How can I be happy when I see my children who are unhappy and starving and cast aside as trash, and despised by those who control the vast wealth of the world, amidst all the treasures I spread among you for the good of all of you? How can it not pain me when I see greedy hoarding all my rich treasures, locked in the banks of the obscenely wealthy, while hundreds of millions of my children starve? There is no sin more hideous than hearts that can turn to ice.

"But one day the judgment and all the roles will be reversed. I am a compassionate God, but I am also a God of justice and my justice is not blind."

A New Look at Violence

Jesus, I am troubled by the word 'violence.' What does violence mean to you?

"Violence is any forceful attack against an obstacle or a person. When I said that 'heaven suffers violence and the violent will carry it away,' I was referring to the violence that a person has to do to himself if he wants to enter the kingdom of heaven, because your inner conflicts are your greatest obstacles.

"There is more violence on earth than is seen with the eyes. The greatest violence is the quiet violence of polished and sophisticated society, violence against the innocent and the unprotected and vulnerable. The violence against them is so smooth and so elegant and refined it passes unnoticed. It is the refined violence that deprives the poor from making a living, and forces them to live isolated from society in crowded ghettoes, far from places where they can find jobs and earn a living, out of the way places where they are out of the sight of the nice people, and where they can quietly die from malnutrition and lack of proper medical attention, and from disease and despair, and where nice people don't have to be burdened with witnessing their daily despair.

199

"The media makes news over people being battered physically, but that is nowhere nearly as bad as violence to a person's soul and heart and self-worth. That is the violence of a spouse and the abuse heaped on his or her partner. That violence is deeper and more destructive than physical violence and is a much greater sin because it attacks the person's soul and destroys the person in the core of his or her personality. So many spouses are destroyed emotionally, psychologically, and spiritually by abusive partners, who demean, belittle, excoriate and berate their spouse on a regular basis, often in front of others. That often hurts and damages more deeply than physical abuse, yet it is overlooked by society's laws.

"The violence of a drunken parent against his or her children and spouse is more destructive of a family's life and of the souls of each one they say they love so much. To say you love and then damage the ones you love with such emotional violence heaps an abuse on the victims that can damage them for years to come, and which will be difficult to erase from their painful memories.

"A wise society will consider the importance of recognizing the injustice done by emotional, psychological, and spiritual violence, because it is principally this kind of violence that breeds dangerous anti-social behavior in later life.

"My message is still the same and more important than ever, 'Love one another as I have loved you,' and that is with kindness, forgiveness, understanding and gentle caring."

"Be happy and never give up your happy spirit for anyone."

Joseph F. Girzone

201

When Confronted with Rude People

Jesus, how should we handle situations with difficult people we work with or mingle with daily?

"Just be up front and simply ask them, 'What's your problem?' and stand and wait for the answer. And if they don't answer just ask, 'Why can't you be nice to people? You make it difficult for everybody when you're miserable. We all try to be nice to you, why don't you return the courtesy?'

"From then on, if the person continues to act like that just walk away and ignore him, and don't show any response. He'll eventually get the point that he's just plain rude. Two of the apostles were like that and I found that that was the only way to treat them. Everyone dislikes being ignored. If they don't like that and walk away, let them go; they'll only be hurting themselves. Eventually they'll learn not to be so ignorant.

"That's the charitable way of treating them rather than having a verbal brawl. Usually they have serious personal problems and when they're hurting and twisted inside, it is not easy to speak and act normal with others. It's hard to talk nice when you have a splitting headache or excruciating pain from a damaged nerve in your back. But then, there are persons who are just plain rude. You can treat them all in the same way. It's the kind way of reacting."

"Holiness and beauty of soul
is more brilliant than
the light of the sun
and its ability to heal and
inspire is awesome."

Joseph F. Girzone

It Was Jesus Who Said: You Cannot Serve God and Money

Jesus, the subject of justice keeps entering my thoughts.

"That has always been the most critical problem throughout history. The whole of history can be reduced to the struggle of people craving power and wealth and their endless schemes to strip others of what is theirs until eventually only a few control societies and the rest are slaves and peasants. Then come the revolutions, as you can see in the Middle East, and have seen with the rise of Communism, and will soon see in the now dominant cultures that are blind to the subtle, but insidious injustices that reign in democracies, where the wealthy and the powerful skillfully rape the masses of their precious rights and possessions. That kind of injustice breeds discontent and social flare-ups, dangerous portents of future unrest. Learn to interpret the signs of the times. If you don't there will be no way to prevent impending catastrophe. The two poles in democratic societies will always be those who struggle for the working people and the vulnerable and those who struggle to control money and power. People must learn to discern the truth beneath all the deceitful propaganda."

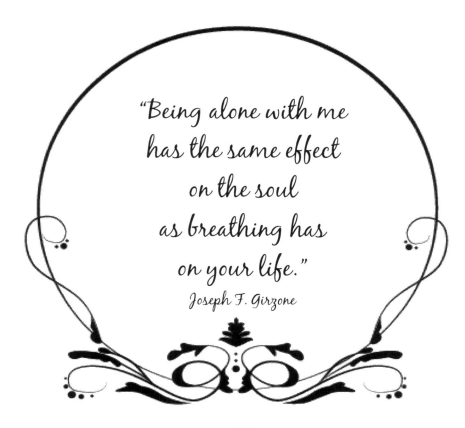

"Being alone with me
has the same effect
on the soul
as breathing has
on your life."

Joseph F. Girzone

What Is Divine Wisdom?

Jesus, I know what it means to be wise and to have wisdom, but what is your kind of wisdom?

"Wisdom is a gift. It is the fruit of a mind and heart that listens, that is open to the whispering voice of the Holy Spirit. There are not very many who have the Wisdom that comes from the Spirit because there are few who are quiet enough to listen.

"The Wisdom that comes from the Spirit enters into the mind of God, and hears the Word that comes from the Father, and begins to understand the Father, and the Father's mind, and in the Word learns to see and understand the inner life of the Father and the Father's vision of creation, and all that is important to the Father. That is why only a person with the Wisdom that comes from the Spirit can understand the Word. I am the Word and it is the role of the Spirit to mold my image in those whom the Spirit draws close to me. In time, Wisdom so completely possesses the soul so blest that it can reflect and interpret and understand the delicate movements between the Father and the Word and the Spirit.

"And it is not just the mind of the Father that Wisdom reveals, but also the infinite love of the Father and the love that is shared through the Spirit. So In the intimacy with which Wisdom anoints the soul, the soul begins to come alive with the love that flows from the divine love and reaches out through that soul to all it touches by its presence.

"All are called to that Wisdom, but few are willing to take the time to listen. That is why listening is the best kind of prayer."

All of Creation Is Related

Jesus, the whole Gospel story is about relationships. It seems your whole life is about relationships.

"Everyone and everything in creation is about relationships. Everything is related, even down to the tiniest elements and their relationships with other elements in forming compounds and all the building blocks of my universe. Everything and everyone depends on one another. That is why it is important to me that your relationships be genuine and sincere, and not just a pretense. The Galileans were with me for half my public life, not because they loved me, but because I was their daily entertainment, healing their sick and crippled, and feeding them when they were hungry. But when I promised them myself as the food of their souls, they laughed at me and walked away in disgust. Their friendship was just a pretense. When I asked the apostles if they were going to leave too, Peter said, 'Lord, where are we going to go. You have the words of eternal life, and (even though we can't understand what you're talking about), we believe in you.' The apostles were true friends, though at that point Judas' heart turned.

"There are all kinds of friends, and there are some who are so centered on themselves that they do not know what friendship is. Some act like friends for what they can get from others. True friends never think of what others can do for them, but always think of how they can enrich their friends' lives. They think of their friends frequently every day, and want only what is good for them. Their love and friendship is genuine and sincere. True friends stand by their friends in good times and in difficult and painful and dangerous times, because their friendship is real, and not make believe. No matter how many friends a true friend has they are always on his or her mind. A good shepherd knows each one of his sheep and watches each one to make sure they are strong and healthy. If one is sick or wanders, he spares no diligence in his concern for that troubled sheep. My consecrated shepherds—if they are good shepherds—will carry the burden and troubles of their sheep on their hearts, day and night. I am the True Shepherd whose flock is spread throughout the whole world. I know each of my sheep by name and know every detail of the life of each one because I love them, and I watch over them and care for them. There is not one thing that happens to them that I am not aware of. They are mine and I hold them close to me. That is the kind of love I want you all to have for one another. Let your love be real and not a pretense."

Come, Be with Me

Jesus, what is important for us to know?

"It is important for people to know how essential it is for them to be alone with me. No one wants to be alone with me, even though it is necessary for their souls. **Being alone with me has the same effect on the soul as breathing has on your life. You** cannot grow spiritually if you do not take time away from the busy-ness of your life to be with me, so you can come to know me and allow me to share with you my ideas about your life, your work, your relationships, and your relationship with me.

"Spending time alone with me is like a ship's captain consulting the instruments on his ship so he can get his bearings during a storm and can make the adjustments he needs to maneuver his way through the violence all around him. Otherwise, he will be like a ship without a rudder, helplessly being tossed about by conflicting winds and raging waters. The most the ship can do is float about aimlessly going nowhere or at worst, backwards, wasting precious time and in the process, being defeated and possibly destroyed.

"I don't ask anyone to spend a lot of time with me, just a few minutes every now and then, so we can share with each other. I understand your life and how complicated it is. You have no idea what is really happening all around you and all the things threatening you continually. I know all the details of the problems that people and situations present for you, and you need my help and guidance to enlighten and protect you."

The Future of the World Is in Its Poor, not Its Rich

Jesus, what is the solution for our country's and the world's problems?

"Treat the poor with respect and justice. So many Christian politicians call them lazy trash. How you treat the poor is how I see you treating me. I have placed talent and genius in the poor, and none of you has the faith deep enough to understand why I keep insisting that you honor them. You think your future lies with the rich. How false! The rich take care only of themselves. It is a rare few who think of others. They will never be the answer to your country's dreams. The sooner you learn to believe and invest in the hidden treasure of the poor, the sooner you will experience a massive burst of creativity and prosperity. That's where your greatest talent for future inventions and discoveries lie. Open your eyes and open your hearts!"

A Most Troubling Affliction Threatening Our World

Jesus, what is the worst problem facing people today?

"Loneliness. Too many people bring on their own loneliness by centering their life on themselves. It is surprising how many people choose not to love but to live their lives for pleasure or for what life and others can do for them. When people like that befriend someone, it is not out love or for healthy comradeship but because they know they can use that person for something they need or to help them do something they have planned, or to increase their business. When they finish using them they drop them, and hardly recognize them later.

"To love means to care. To care means thinking about others. One of the most insidious problems facing society is the number of people who refuse to love, and if they do love, it is not sincere and based on caring. They make the conscious decision not to love because love is painful, and demanding, and presses a person to think of others, not just occasionally but as a constant part of your life. It means giving up your own comfort when a friend needs you, and when you would rather do things you enjoy doing. It means getting beneath a person's strange behavior and understanding what is troubling someone. It means always being there when a loved one is hurting and needs your help. It means not destroying a competitor but to compete in a friendly way, and at times, helping each other to improve each other's endeavors. It means in politics, and especially in international politics, looking upon leaders of other nations not as potential enemies but as partners who have needs for their own people, and having the humility and bigness of heart to reach out and try to resolve complex situations in a reasonable and mutually beneficial way.

"Love and caring among people is becoming a lost art today, as too many people, especially people in important positions, choose to live in psychological prison cells where they think of themselves all day long and care little about the needs and dreams of others. For them, reaching out to others is a show of weakness and need and reaching out to competitors, especially competing foreign leaders, as servile appeasement. Arrogance and bullying is their stock in trade. The unfortunate outcome of such behavior is that nothing is every accomplished, and wounds are never healed, and tensions are never lessened. Irrational and costly preparations for armed conflict for many years in advance are the self-destructive by-product of such behavior.

"If the world is to have peace, people must learn to love first, and to sincerely care for others. Peace then just happens. You can't look upon everybody with suspicion and always prepare for war, and expect to have peace. One cancels out the other."

"If the world is to have peace,
people have to learn
to love first, and to
sincerely care for others.
Peace then just happens.
Joseph F. Girzone

God's Universal Knowledge

Jesus, how can God know every detail of everything that happens to every human being throughout the universe all at the same time?

"Very simply. It is sort of like you being aware of every little detail of everything that touches you and causes you pain or pleasure, or even just the feeling of a tiny insect landing on one part of your skin, or even a number of sensations happening to your body at any particular time. You are aware of them all because your consciousness is present in every part of your body. I am present throughout all creation and I am aware of every slight change or happening in every part of the universe. Every tiny change has meaning to me, especially when change affects any one of you who are so precious to me. Nothing escapes my attention. I know of every good thing no matter how important or unimportant, and every evil thing no matter how important or unimportant that happens to each one of you. I am aware immediately, and I am always present to respond when you need me. So never be afraid, or think that I have forgotten you. Nothing that happens to you escapes my attention and my concern. And, I don't sleep, so don't worry!"

Great Puppet Master

Jesus, are you like the great puppet master who pulls all the strings that control our lives and makes things happen?

"When we created the world and the beginning of the human family, we made all things perfect, and the human family was endowed with unlimited freedom to make decisions. We blessed you with the freedom to live your own lives, follow your own dreams, make your own mistakes, and gave you all the tools you needed to survive and prosper. We respected the freedom we gave you and did not interfere in how you lived your lives.

"Today we all live with the world you have fashioned by all the decisions made throughout your history. It could have been a beautiful world you created, but instead we are faced with a massive mess, with more than half the human family starving and on the verge of despair. By your tinkering with, and abusing the genetic blueprints we designed for the gradual and continuous development of your lives, you have created a nightmare that breeds accidents and often fatal illnesses that we had hoped would never happen. And then you turn around and blame it on God.

"Little did you know how many times we reached out and made adjustments to save the lives of so many whom you have damaged by your thoughtless or selfish schemes. We never interfered or punished you or harmed you in any way. We treated you only with goodness and endless blessings, continuously prodding you and inspiring you to do things differently. But, our voice and our promptings fell on deaf ears and cold hearts, which made us wonder if we erred in giving you the freedom to oppose the God who made you.

"Now we look at the mess you have made and hear your constant complaining that it's my fault that there is so much evil in the world. And you say so often, 'If God is supposed to be so good, why is there such evil and hatred and sickness and disease and innocent people dying?

"Look in the mirror and you will see the real cause of all this evil. I gave you only rich treasures and talents and the ability to dream. But all you dreamed about was power over others, amassing great wealth, building vast armies to destroy those who oppose you, exploiting and raping my creation for all its treasures to satisfy your greed, and leaving the people poor and helpless after stealing all their resources. Then, you have the impudence to blame the world's evils on me? You are fortunate I even allow you to exist.

"So, my friend, you still ask me if I am the great puppet master. No, it seems I am the world's greatest fool for loving you and trusting you so much."

Greater Accessibility Is Needed for the Spiritually, Emotionally and Psychologically Disabled

Jesus, it must bring you joy when you see so many elderly finding their way back to visit you because your churches are so accessible with all the new additions.

"Those elderly people have always been faithful, and I find joy that the churches are more accessible. But, that is only a first step. What really troubles me are the vast number, the overwhelming majority of my people, men and women, who have been disabled and crippled in spirit by the damage done to them often since childhood. These are the ones who have been broken in spirit, damaged physically, emotionally, psychologically and spiritually by fathers and mothers, brothers and sisters, uncles, aunts and relatives and those they trusted. Among them are so many women, and some men, who find it near impossible for them to call God, 'Father,' because of things done to them by their earthly fathers, and so many who have been broken by abuse of all sorts inflicted on them. Many cringe at the thought of me embracing them because they have learned not to trust men.

"What it is that troubles me is that when they finally find the courage and the humility to come back to church to draw close to me, they are told they are not yet ready to be embraced by me. There are many things they must do first before they are worthy of my embrace. I cannot express how abhorrent that is to me that clergy dare to tell these damaged and helpless sheep that I am not ready to embrace them. Don't they realize that that is the kind of accessibility in my church that I demand—accessibility for the spiritually and emotionally disabled? Rather than making me more accessible to them, they add obstacles that make it almost impossible for people to approach me. It is like finding a lost sheep, bringing it home, and then saying, 'Now, you go and sit in the corner while the rest of us have supper. 'Don't they realize that I gave my Flesh and Blood to Judas at the Last Supper—my last attempt to draw him close to me. Eucharist is not just a reward for holiness; it is medicine for the sick and despairing. When will my shepherds wake up and learn to read my heart? I have always reached out to embrace sinners. Eucharist is my embrace of those who have been lost. I don't want to continue losing them because of careless shepherds."

Unhealthy Resistance to Truth

Jesus, what was your most troublesome problem in dealing with people?

"Feeling unable to communicate. That may seem odd to you because I am God and can easily control people's minds. But, I never played tricks like that. I was always in every way human in my dealings with people. My pain came from the reality that my mind is filled only with pure truth, with a clarity that can penetrate the most complex and obscure problems. As simple as I tried to be with people I found that even the simplest things I said were rejected. I could see it in their faces. Whatever I said seemed to mystify them. Looking into their minds I could see that truth was difficult to find in all that they believed. Their minds were cluttered with untruths and prejudices, lies about others, untrue gossip passed around by friends and family, false teachings spread by scribes and wandering Pharisees, religious tales that were the opposite of what my Father tried to teach through the prophets. They felt so comfortable with all these things they clung to all their lives; they did not want to accept what I tried to teach them because it made them feel uncomfortable and insecure. They treasured their prejudices and all the lies they had made a part of themselves, and what I said was foreign.

"What I did notice is that when I said something that made them feel good about themselves, they accepted it because they saw it as absolving them from guilt they had harbored for years. But when I said something that was new to them or treated kindly someone they hated, they became furious with me, especially when I picked Levi, the publican, the tax collector, to be one of my apostles. The only person I could share with and she could share with me was the Samaritan woman at the well. What I said shocked her, especially when I said 'Salvation is from the Jews,' but she was willing to continue talking with me and we had a lively conversation. Most people would cut me off when I tried to talk about a subject that made them uncomfortable. But, the Samaritan woman was a special person. She didn't hold her prejudiced beliefs as off limits. She was willing to accept the possibility that she could be wrong, and in the end accepted what I said, and ran to tell others that she had found truth. In her honesty, she brought that whole community to faith, and they ended up being among my first followers.

"But, she was rare. Most people resent being freed of their mistaken beliefs and their dangerous prejudices, like the Galileans who had wanted to make me king when I multiplied the loaves and fishes and impressed them with my power, then turned against me in disgust the next day when I told them I would give them my flesh and blood as the food from heaven which would be their pledge of eternal salvation. They turned away from me never to return. I refused to tell them how I would do it, but I had already given them reason enough to have faith that when I promised something, it would be reasonable.

"That was my greatest problem with people. Their minds were so full of erroneous beliefs and falsehoods, that my truth made them uncomfortable. Even the apostles did not understand me. It was only their attachment to me that made them cling to our friendship. But, even they were dense and until after my resurrection they still had a difficult time believing in what I said. They clung to the end with what they had been taught by others since childhood. That problem of communicating truth to humans was extremely painful, and made me feel very much alone in the world. My only comfort was the nights I spent in the hills with my Father, with whom I could pour out my heart and be understood."

The Short Story of the Drama of Redemption

Jesus, there is a big controversy raging over Adam and Eve, and whether they were real people and our first parents.

"Whoever among the priests and scribes wrote down those long-told stories passed down for centuries at family gatherings did not do a very thorough job. They left many unanswered questions and much room of doubt and controversy. What is important is that the earliest human beings we created asserted their independence from my Father, and chose to live the way they wanted regardless of whether it pleased my Father or not. In doing that they cut us out of their lives, and opened themselves to the cunning schemes of Satan, who ruled among them for many, many thousands of years.

"What is important for you to know is that I came down from heaven to take upon myself the burden of your sins, and not just yours, but the sins of the entire world from the beginning of the human family. In taking upon myself your sins, I became your living and true Lamb of God, offering himself in your name and in the name of all from the beginning of the human race until the present day to atone for all your sins, and what is more important, drawing down upon you a sharing in my divine life, so that one day you could be with me in heaven for all eternity. When I shared my life with you in baptism I lifted you from the mere creature level, into the rarified level of the supernatural, and into my family, so you could have the ability one day to see us in the way we see you, and so we could share with you our life in the heavenly kingdom. And even now you share in our life in a way that makes it possible for us to communicate with each other in beautiful intimacy.

"That basically is the drama of redemption, and a beautiful love story between God and his human family."

Wandering Aimlessly

Jesus, we seem to be living in a strange world, a world in which people seem lost and without purpose.

"That's because you have become a world without faith. Even people who think they are people of faith and talk about faith and preach faith, do not really believe in faith. Your senseless obsession with your economy reflects distraction from real values I have taught. Your resentment over the existence of the poor in your midst, and your refusal to help them reflects your lack of faith and real acceptance of all that I have taught about the sacredness of the poor. Your excessive passion for material wealth and possessions reflects your lack of faith in the values that I have taught you. Your use of the talents and gifts I have given you to help others and to make your community a better place to live, you keep for yourselves and use to enrich yourselves and your friends. Your resorting to war to solve problems shows not only lack of faith, but your lack of trust in my care and even my power to protect you and assist you in solving problems with others. The ones who talk most about their loyalty to me and their country are the very ones who have lost sight of the real values that I taught, because they are not authentic Christians. Their loyalty and faith is focused on the image of me they have created for themselves, and a Christ they feel comfortable with. Unfortunately, it is a sad and sickly caricature of who I am and how I really think and love.

"Until your world finally decides to accept the real Jesus, and not the Jesus they created, you will continue to walk around in the dark. Faith is like a compass, pointing the direction, and like a highly advanced directional system showing each step along the way. When you finally make up your minds to lay aside your material dreams, then you might be ready to accept me. Until then you will still wander aimlessly."

Quotes from the book "Joshua's Reflections" by Joseph F. Girzone.

Original Source: Page 58
Highlighted on Page 8
"It is much easier to reflect the simplicity and beauty of Jesus when we walk freely through the world unattended to things."

Original Source: Page 35
Highlighted on Page 12
 "An attitude of self-importance destroys that humility that is necessary for a person to be a vehicle of a divine mission."

Original Source: Page 106
Highlighted on Page 20
"I have given you all you need to live happy lives. I want more than anything that you be happy."

Original Source: Page 35
Highlighted on Page 28
"To know what comes from the heart of God, they must be humble to receive that understanding."

Original Source: Page 68
Highlighted on Page 41
"Banish your fear of the future. It will be brighter than you can imagine. I am still in control and I am with you always."

Original Source: Page 151
Highlighted on Page 59
"Love has to be the engine that drives the world if the world is to be healthy and prosperous. Teach the world to love."

Original Source: Page 61
Highlighted on Page 62
"The whole world is finding itself shrinking, as people learn to realize how much they need each other."

Original Source: Page 93
Highlighted on Page 64
"Trust me, I am with you, and have everything under control."

Original Source: Page 97
Highlighted on Page 66
"You will find a peace that is beyond all earthly treasures and in that peace, a joy beyond measure."

Original Source: Page 79
Highlighted on Page 86
"I am a living, vibrant and exciting reality full of life and joy and wanting so much to be a living part of your lives."

Original Source: Page 97
Highlighted on Page 109
"Do not be afraid to open your heart to the Holy Spirit so he can fill your life with his blessings."

Original Source: Page 107
Highlighted on Page 112
"That bond between us forges a warm partnership which allows me and the Holy Spirit to use you as an instrument of accomplishing wonderful things."

Original Source: Page 110
Highlighted on Page 124
"You reflect God by your intelligence and will, your ability to think and to love."

Original Source: Page 142
Highlighted on Page 129
"Anyone who tries to follow in my footsteps and live the way I live will experience the same rejection and ridicule."

Original Source: Page 151
Highlighted on Page 150
"The world can only grow when there is love."

Original Source: Page 114
Highlighted on Page 197
"The one thing that is essential for the survival of humanity is love."

Original Source: Page 180
Highlighted on Page 202
"Be happy and never give up your happy spirit for anyone."

Original Source: Page 155
Highlighted on Page 204
"Holiness and beauty of soul is more brilliant than the light of the sun and it ability to heal and inspire is awesome."

Original Source: Page 210
Highlighted on Page 206
"Being alone with me has the same effect on the soul as breathing."

Original Source: Page 214
Highlighted on Page 216
"If the world is to have peace, people have to learn to love first, and to sincerely care for others. Peace then just happens."

41988883R00129

Made in the USA
Middletown, DE
28 March 2017